PRESIDENT'S MALARIA INITIATIVE

Guinea

Malaria Operational Plan FY 2016

TABLE OF CONTENTS

ABBREVIATIONS and ACRONYMS

AS-AQ	Artesunate-amodiaquine
AL	Artemether lumefantrine
ACT	Artemisinin-based combination therapy
ANC	Antenatal care
BCC	Behavior change communication
CDC	Centers for Disease Control and Prevention
CHW	Community health worker
CM	Case Management
DHS	Demographic Health Survey
DNPL	National Directorate of Pharmacies and Laboratory
EPI	Expanded program on immunization
EU	European Union
EUV	End-use verification
FY	Fiscal year
Global Fund	Global Fund to Fight AIDS, Tuberculosis and Malaria
GOG	Government of Guinea
HCW	Health care worker
HMIS	Health Management Information System
KAP	Knowledge, Attitudes, and Practices survey
IDB	Islamic Development Bank
IRS	Indoor residual spraying
IPTp	Intermittent preventive treatment for pregnant women
ITN	Insecticide-treated mosquito net
JICA	Japan International Cooperation Agency
KAP	Knowledge Attitude and Practice
LMIS	Logistic Management Information System
M&E	Monitoring and evaluation
MICS	Multiple Indicator Cluster Survey
MIP	Malaria in pregnancy
MIS	Malaria Indicator Survey
MOH	Ministry of Health and Public Hygiene
NMCP	National Malaria Control Program
NGO	Non-governmental organization
OMVS	Organization of the Development of the Senegal River
PCG	Central Pharmacy of Guinea
PMI	President's Malaria Initiative
RBM	Roll Back Malaria
RDT	Rapid Diagnostic Test
SARA	Service Availability and Readiness Assessment
SP	Sulfadoxine-pyrimethamine
USAID	United States Agency for International Development
UNICEF	United Nations Children's Fund
WHO	World Health Organization

I. EXECUTIVE SUMMARY

When it was launched in 2005, the goal of the President's Malaria Initiative (PMI) was to reduce malaria-related mortality by 50% across 15 high-burden countries in sub-Saharan Africa through a rapid scale-up of four proven and highly effective malaria prevention and treatment measures: insecticide-treated mosquito nets (ITNs); indoor residual spraying (IRS); accurate diagnosis and prompt treatment with artemisinin-based combination therapies (ACTs); and intermittent preventive treatment of pregnant women (IPTp). With the passage of the Tom Lantos and Henry J. Hyde Global Leadership against HIV/AIDS, Tuberculosis, and Malaria Act in 2008, PMI developed a U.S. Government Malaria Strategy for 2009–2014. This strategy included a long-term vision for malaria control in which sustained high coverage with malaria prevention and treatment interventions would progressively lead to malaria-free zones in Africa, with the ultimate goal of worldwide malaria eradication by 2040-2050. Consistent with this strategy and the increase in annual appropriations supporting PMI, four new sub-Saharan African countries and one regional program in the Greater Mekong Subregion of Southeast Asia were added in 2011. The contributions of PMI, together with those of other partners, have led to dramatic improvements in the coverage of malaria control interventions in PMI-supported countries, and all 15 original countries have documented substantial declines in all-cause mortality rates among children less than five years of age.

In 2015, PMI launched the next six-year strategy, setting forth a bold and ambitious goal and objectives. The PMI Strategy 2015-2020 takes into account the progress over the past decade and the new challenges that have arisen. Malaria prevention and control remains a major U.S. foreign assistance objective and PMI's Strategy fully aligns with the U.S. Government's vision of ending preventable child and maternal deaths and ending extreme poverty. It is also in line with the goals articulated in the RBM Partnership's second generation global malaria action plan, *Action and Investment to defeat Malaria (AIM) 2016-2030: for a Malaria-Free World* and WHO's updated *Global Technical Strategy: 2016-2030*. Under the PMI Strategy 2015-2020, the U.S. Government's goal is to work with PMI-supported countries and partners to further reduce malaria deaths and substantially decrease malaria morbidity, towards the long-term goal of elimination.

Guinea was selected as a PMI focus country in FY 2011.

This FY 2016 Malaria Operational Plan presents a detailed implementation plan for Guinea, based on the strategies of PMI and the National Malaria Control Program (NMCP). It was developed in consultation with the NMCP and with the participation of national and international partners involved in malaria prevention and control in the country. The activities that PMI is proposing to support fit in well with the National Malaria Control strategy and plan and build on investments made by PMI and other partners to improve and expand malaria-related services, including the Global Fund to Fight AIDS, Tuberculosis, and Malaria (Global Fund) malaria grants. This document briefly reviews the current status of malaria control policies and interventions in Guinea, describes progress to date, identifies challenges and unmet needs to achieving the targets of the NMCP and PMI, and provides a description of activities that are planned with FY 2016 funding.

The proposed FY 2016 PMI budget for Guinea is $12.5 million. PMI will support the following intervention areas with these funds:

Insecticide-treated nets (ITNs): The national malaria strategy is to support free distribution of long lasting insecticide-treated nets through antenatal care (ANC) and vaccination clinics; free distribution through mass campaigns; and the sale of ITNs in the commercial sector in order to reach 80% coverage by the end of 2017. PMI contributed approximately 1.75 million ITNs to the first universal coverage campaign, which took place between May 2013 and May 2014. PMI delivered 180,000 ITNs for routine use and procured an additional 235,000 for delivery in 2015. With FY 2016 funds PMI will procure and distribute approximately 600,000 LLINs for routine service delivery, and promote correct and consistent use of ITNs throughout the year.

Indoor residual spraying (IRS): The national malaria strategy includes IRS, but this activity is not currently implemented by the government. Limited spraying in the country is carried out by mining companies, which spray work sites and surrounding areas. Current PMI support is being used to conduct standard entomological surveillance including species identification and insecticide resistance, and to build capacity of key personnel to conduct and manage an entomological surveillance program. With FY 2016 funds PMI will continue to support surveillance and support skills building within the NMCP and other national structures to conduct entomologic surveillance. Additionally, PMI will support the maintenance of the national insectary.

Malaria in pregnancy (MIP): The national malaria strategy includes the administration of intermittent preventive treatment in pregnancy (IPTp) with sulfadoxine-pyrimethamine (SP) under the direct observation of an ANC attendant, at four-week intervals, starting in the second trimester (starting from week 13), with at least three treatments given before delivery; the provision of an ITN at the time of the first visit; and prompt diagnosis and treatment of malaria during pregnancy. PMI's support includes procuring and distributing SP and ITNs, training and supervision of health workers, and communication activities to promote IPTp uptake and ITN use among pregnant women. In the past year, PMI procured and distributed 375,000 treatments of SP, 180,000 ITNs, trained over 1,000 health workers, and revised MIP tools, guidelines and protocols, aligning them with WHO recommendations. With FY 2016 funds PMI will procure and distribute 1,565,000 treatments of SP to cover 100% of the national need, train health workers, and promote IPTp uptake and ITN use via communication efforts.

Case management: The national malaria strategy and policy recommends diagnostic confirmation of all suspected malaria cases, among all patients, with either microscopy (when available) or a rapid diagnostic test (RDT), before they are treated with an ACT (artesunate-amodiaquine [AS-AQ]or artemether-lumefantrine [AL]) for simple malaria or injectable artesunate, artemether, or quinine for severe malaria. The policy includes community-case management, whereby trained, community health workers administer an RDT and dispense an ACT upon positive confirmation. Pregnant women in their first trimester with uncomplicated malaria are to be treated with oral quinine; in the second and third trimesters, they are to be treated with ACT. The national policy is to deliver malaria treatment and prevention commodities through the public system via the *Pharmacie Centrale de Guinée* (PCG). In the past year PMI procured and distributed 5 million RDTs, 2 million ACTs and 69,000 treatments of injectable artesunate. In the context of Ebola, NMCP revised the case management guideline based on the WHO recommendations, supported training of health workers about differential diagnosis, and is reviewing malaria commodity consumption to rationalize future procurements in collaboration with the PCG and the NMCP. With FY 2016 funds PMI will procure and distribute 4.16 million RDTs, 2 million treatments of ACTs, support community case management efforts, reinforce PCG and strengthen the supply chain down to the facility level.

Health systems strengthening and capacity building: Even before the Ebola epidemic was declared in March 2014, Guinea's health system faced important challenges; among the most critical were the management capacity of the NMCP and limited human resources for health. One year into the epidemic and the situation is even worse, with health worker attrition (due to health worker death, migration to Ebola activities, or abandonment of service because of fear) being the most obvious capacity limitation the country is facing. During the past year, PMI supported the training of 1,675 health workers and 680 community health workers (CHWs) in case management, including differential diagnosis of malaria and Ebola. PMI support helped organize supervision for 14 district teams to visit the health facilities under their purview. Finally, PMI support assisted the NMCP to reactivate the various technical working groups they manage. With FY 2016 funds, PMI will continue to build the capacity of the NMCP by facilitating participation in training sessions. PMI support will also support operations of the NMCP offices, including communications.

Behavior change communication (BCC): The NMCP's malaria communication plan emphasizes appropriate strategies and channels to reach various target groups with culturally appropriate messaging on malaria prevention and control. A BCC Technical Working Group, established in the past year, oversees BCC activities and provides guidance and approval for changes based on current information and data. As part of the Ebola response, new or revised messages were developed to help both health workers and communities to deal with the epidemic while maintaining focus on malaria interventions. PMI was instrumental in messaging concerning correct and consistent use of ITNs as part of post distribution campaigns. Finally, PMI supported a Knowledge, Attitudes and Practices (KAP) survey, the results of which will help guide revision of messaging and dissemination tools. With FY 2016 funds, PMI will continue to support the NMCP's communication plan with implementation of BCC activities reflecting NMCP priorities and national policies, including ITN use, ANC attendance and IPTp uptake, and case management, including RDT and ACT use, as well as malaria case management in the context of Ebola.

Monitoring and evaluation (M&E): The national malaria M&E plan identifies indicators, targets, and data sources and emphasizes data collection, data quality assurance, and dissemination and use of data. A monthly malaria reporting form is currently being used throughout the country, and completion rates have been improving. Starting October 2014, the NMCP began issuing monthly malaria bulletins, summarizing the malaria epidemiological situation in the country and presenting key indicators for each health district. The Malaria Indicator Survey (MIS) planned for 2014 was postponed (indefinitely) due to the Ebola epidemic. However, a planned KAP survey was carried out in PMI target zones in September 2014. Moreover, as a response to anecdotal reports of falling health facility attendance in the context of the Ebola epidemic, a health facility survey was conducted in December 2014 to assess the impact of Ebola on malaria services. In addition, two end-use verification (EUV) surveys were carried out, providing valuable information on current supplies of malaria prevention and treatment commodities. With FY 2016 funds, PMI will continue to support twice-yearly EUV surveys, a health facility survey, ongoing therapeutic efficacy studies, strengthening of routine data quality including use of data for decision-making, and a full malaria module for the 2017 Demographic and Health Survey (DHS).

II. STRATEGY

1. Introduction

When it was launched in 2005, the goal of PMI was to reduce malaria-related mortality by 50% across 15 high-burden countries in sub-Saharan Africa through a rapid scale-up of four proven and highly effective malaria prevention and treatment measures: insecticide-treated mosquito nets (ITNs); indoor residual spraying (IRS); accurate diagnosis and prompt treatment with artemisinin-based combination therapies (ACTs); and intermittent preventive treatment of pregnant women (IPTp). With the passage of the Tom Lantos and Henry J. Hyde Global Leadership against HIV/AIDS, Tuberculosis, and Malaria Act in 2008, PMI developed a U.S. Government Malaria Strategy for 2009–2014. This strategy included a long-term vision for malaria control in which sustained high coverage with malaria prevention and treatment interventions would progressively lead to malaria-free zones in Africa, with the ultimate goal of worldwide malaria eradication by 2040-2050. Consistent with this strategy and the increase in annual appropriations supporting PMI, four new sub-Saharan African countries and one regional program in the Greater Mekong Subregion of Southeast Asia were added in 2011. The contributions of PMI, together with those of other partners, have led to dramatic improvements in the coverage of malaria control interventions in PMI-supported countries, and all 15 original countries have documented substantial declines in all-cause mortality rates among children less than five years of age.

In 2015, PMI launched the next six-year strategy, setting forth a bold and ambitious goal and objectives. The PMI Strategy for 2015-2020 takes into account the progress over the past decade and the new challenges that have arisen. Malaria prevention and control remains a major U.S. foreign assistance objective and PMI's Strategy fully aligns with the U.S. Government's vision of ending preventable child and maternal deaths and ending extreme poverty. It is also in line with the goals articulated in the RBM Partnership's second generation global malaria action plan, *Action and Investment to defeat Malaria (AIM) 2016-2030: for a Malaria-Free World* and WHO's updated *Global Technical Strategy: 2016-2030*. Under the PMI Strategy 2015-2020, the U.S. Government's goal is to work with PMI-supported countries and partners to further reduce malaria deaths and substantially decrease malaria morbidity, towards the long-term goal of elimination.

Guinea was selected as a PMI focus country in FY 2011.

Guinea is highly endemic for malaria. In a 2012 national survey, malaria infection prevalence in children <5 was 44% nationwide[1]. Malaria is the main cause of health facility visits in Guinea, responsible for over 30% of all public health facility visits.[2] A pillar of the National Malaria Control Program's efforts to reduce malaria morbidity and mortality is the expansion of access to malaria diagnostics, most commonly in the form of rapid diagnostic tests (RDTs), and antimalarial treatments in the form of artemisinin-based combination therapy (ACT) for

---

[1] Institut National de la Statistique (INS) and ICF International. 2012. Guinea Demographic and Health Survey 2012. Conakry, Guinea
[2] National Malaria Control Strategy 2013-2017

8

uncomplicated malaria and parenteral treatment with artemisinin derivatives for severe malaria. Access to ACTs and RDTs is provided through public health facilities and a network of over 3,000 community health workers (CHWs), each supplied and supervised from a health center.

Large-scale implementation of ACTs and IPTp began in 2011 and has progressed rapidly with support from PMI and other partners. Rapid diagnostic tests, ACTs, and sulfadoxine-pyrimethamine (SP) for IPTp are now available across the country in public health facilities. In addition to over 5 million long-lasting ITNs distributed through a mass distribution campaign in 2013 and early 2014, a new routine nets distribution has started targeting pregnant women in antenatal clinics and children under one year of age in immunization clinics.

PMI activities in Guinea were progressing very well until the Ebola epidemic started. This unprecedented epidemic began in December 2013 but was first detected and declared in March 2014[3]. As of March 24th, 2015 an estimated 3459 cases of which 2,273 deaths were reported in Guinea[4]

The Ebola epidemic curve has so far been characterized by four successive waves, the first from December 2013 to March 2014, the second from April to July 2014, the third from August 2014 to January 2015 and the fourth, currently ongoing wave starting in February 2015. While the first two waves were localized in Conakry and in the forest region, the third and the fourth waves have affected most of Guinea. At the start of the third wave in August 2014, the National Malaria Control Program (NMCP) began to receive reports of falling attendance in health facilities and reductions in community agent's malaria activities. The NMCP commissioned a nationwide health facility survey, complemented by an analysis of routine malaria surveillance data, to evaluate the impact of Ebola on malaria activities. The survey was conducted in December 2014 and showed a drastic reduction in health facilities attendance both for all causes and fever cases as well as a drop in the number of cases of suspect malaria treated by antimalarial drugs. This reduction was significantly more pronounced in Ebola-affected prefectures compared with unaffected prefectures[5].

The impact of Ebola epidemic on the Guinean healthcare system includes a change in patients' health seeking behavior and the ultimate delivery of health care, in particular in malaria activities because of the overlap of malaria and Ebola symptoms, and malaria control efforts' dependence on case management delivered at, or coordinated through, health facilities. There are concerns that the indirect effects of the Ebola epidemic on malaria care delivery could ultimately be responsible for more morbidity and mortality than was due to malaria in previous years before PMI programming started and more than morbidity and mortality due to the Ebola virus disease. The impact of Ebola on the overall health system will also impact indirectly malaria interventions and divert political attention from malaria.

---

[3] Official declaration of Ebola epidemic by the Government of Guinea on the 21 of March 2014 after notification of a laboratory-confirmed Ebola epidemic in Guinea to WHO in accordance with the International Health Regulations (IHR 2005)
[4] Ebola SITREP as of the 25th of March 2015, WHO.
[5]Plucinski, M, Guilavogui, T, Sidikiba, S., et al. Substantial impact of the Ebola epidemic on malaria case management in Guinea, Under Review. 2015

Guinea is facing a unique challenge of trying to revive malaria activities in a country affected by an ongoing Ebola epidemic. This includes effectively implementing the new guidelines on malaria case management in the context of Ebola, adjusting NMCP recommendations and efforts in the context of the Ebola epidemic, and promoting infection control in health facilities by providing personal equipment material to health workers to be able to perform examination of patients, RDTs testing for suspect malaria cases and providing care to patients.

This FY 2016 Malaria Operational Plan presents a detailed implementation plan for Guinea, based on the strategies of PMI and the National Malaria Control Program (NMCP) strategy. It was developed in consultation with the NMCP and with the participation of national and international partners involved in malaria prevention and control in the country. The activities that PMI is proposing to support fit in well with the National Malaria Control strategy and plan and build on investments made by PMI and other partners to improve and expand malaria-related services, including the Global Fund to Fight AIDS, Tuberculosis, and Malaria (Global Fund) malaria grants. This document briefly reviews the current status of malaria control policies and interventions in Guinea, describes progress to date, identifies challenges and unmet needs to achieving the targets of the NMCP and PMI, and provides a description of activities that are planned with FY 2016 funding.

2. **Malaria situation in Guinea**

Guinea is a coastal country in West Africa composed of four areas with distinct ecologies: lower Guinea, which includes the coastal lowlands; middle Guinea, the mountainous region running north-south in the middle of the country; the sahelian upper Guinea; and the forested jungle area in the south. Guinea borders Guinea-Bissau and Senegal to the north, Mali and Côte d'Ivoire to the east, and Liberia and Sierra Leone to the south. Guinea has 33 prefectures (districts) divided into eight administrative regions, one of which is the capital city of Conakry and its five communes. Guinea's entire estimated population of 11.7 million people is at risk of malaria. According to the 2014 Human Development Index, Guinea has among the lowest health and development indicators, ranking 179 out of 187 countries[6]. Poverty has been steadily increasing over the past decade and as of 2012 over half (55%) of Guinea's population lives below the World Bank poverty head count ratio.[7]

The overall literacy rate is 41% for adults over 15 years (52% males, 30% females). Infant and under-five mortality rates are 81 and 130 per 1,000 live births, respectively. Although antenatal care (ANC) coverage of at least one visit is high (88%), the percentage of women who make at least two to three visits is still low at 18%. The lifetime risk of maternal death is one of the worst in the world, at 1 in 26. Total expenditure on health per capita is 67 USD and life expectancy at birth is low at 55 years.[7]

Guinea has year-round malaria transmission with peak transmission from July through October in most areas. The two main vectors are *Anopheles gambiae* and *Anopheles funestus*. According to the national strategy, malaria remains the number one public health problem in Guinea, with

---

[6] http://hdr.undp.org/en/content/table-1-human-development-index-and-its-components
[7] http://data.worldbank.org/country/guinea

92% of malaria infections caused by *Plasmodium falciparum* (2012 DHS). The annual incidence rate in 2011 was estimated to be 92 per 1,000. National statistics in Guinea also show that among children less than five years of age, malaria accounts for 31% of consultations, 25% of hospitalizations, and 14% of hospital deaths. This estimate does not include malaria cases seen in the community or in private facilities. Among the general population, malaria is also the primary cause of consultations (34%), hospitalizations (31%), and death (14%) according to the Ministry of Health (MOH).

According to the 2012 Demographic Health Survey (DHS), the prevalence of malaria among children under five years of age ranged between 3% in Conakry and 66% in Faranah with a national prevalence of 44% for children 6-59 months using microscopy, and 47% based on RDT results. Parasitemia prevalence showed strong variations by place of residence with 53% in rural areas compared to 18% in urban areas (strongly influenced by Conakry). The survey results also showed that 77% of children 6-59 months had anemia, and 16% had severe anemia (Hgb<8g/dl)[8].

Coverage estimates for key interventions showed room for improvement in reaching targets. A little more than half of households surveyed had at least one mosquito net, treated or untreated (53%), while 47% of households own at least one ITN. These proportions were somewhat higher in rural areas (55% and 50%) than in urban (48% and 42%). The proportions of children who slept under any mosquito net and under an ITN the night before the survey were 29% and 26%, respectively. These proportions were higher in rural areas (30% and 27%) than in urban (28% and 24%). In households with an ITN, the proportion of children under five years of age who slept under an ITN the night before the survey was 51% with no difference between urban and rural households. One in three pregnant women reported sleeping under any mosquito net (33%) while 28% reported sleeping under an ITN. In households with an ITN, the proportion of pregnant women who slept under an ITN the night before the survey was 59%. This proportion is higher in urban (62%) than rural (58%) areas. Coverage with IRS was relatively low as this intervention was not part of the national malaria control strategy. As a result, limited IRS activities were found to be happening in the country (1.7% of households per year, 2012 DHS), mainly in the mining sector (BHP Biliton, Global Alumina, Vale and RioTinto).

Malaria treatment indicators reflected low coverage; among children less than five years old with fever in the two weeks before the DHS survey, 37% had sought advice or treatment for the fever, 28% had received any antimalarial treatment, and less than 1% received an ACT on the same or next day. Of those children under five with fever that took any antimalarial, only 4.8% of these took an ACT; of the rest, 35.7% took chloroquine, 30.7% took quinine, 23.3% took monotherapy Amodiaquine, 6.0% took SP/Fansidar, and 5.3% took something else.

Since 2005, prevention of malaria among pregnant women using sulfadoxine-pyrimethamine (SP) was included in the national ANC health package with support to the NMCP from several partners. PMI will focus on improving prevention of malaria in pregnancy (MIP) as only 18% of women reported receiving two or more doses of SP during their last pregnancy (2012 DHS).

---

[8] Institut National de la Statistique (INS) and ICF International. 2012. Guinea Demographic and Health Survey 2012. Conakry, Guinea

3. Country health system delivery structure and Ministry of Health (MOH) organization

The health care system in Guinea is managed by the Ministry of Health (MOH) and based on the administrative division of the country into eight regions. Within the 8 regions there are 38 health districts composed of 334 rural municipalities and 38 urban municipalities. The MOH has three levels in its administrative structure: central, intermediate, and peripheral. The health system is organized around a pyramidal structure on three levels:

1. The central level is responsible for the strategic development plan, policy, monitoring and evaluation and resource allocation and includes the cabinet of the Minister of Health (Secretary General, advisers, chief of staff, and support services), National Directorates, and related services (the National Directorate of Pharmacy and Laboratory ,the National Directorate for hospital facilities and care –Hospital Management Board, the National Directorate of Family Health and Nutrition ,the National Directorate of Public Hygiene, the National Directorate of Prevention and Community Health) .

2. The intermediate level: includes the seven Regional Directorates of Health (DRS) plus Conakry Directorate of Health. Within each region there are four sections: prevention and disease control, a regional inspection of the pharmacy and laboratories, administrative and financial section and a hygiene section. Each section or unit is filled by one individual. The prevention and disease control officer alone for instance oversees all diseases within the region. The pharmacist inspector alone oversees all pharmaceutical activities within the region.

3. The peripheral level includes the 38 Prefectural and Municipal Directorates of Health (DPS/DCS). Within each prefecture there is a section of Prevention and Disease Control, as well as lab-pharmacy, planning and training, administrative and financial, and hygiene sections.

The provision of care is provided by the public and private sectors. Public health facilities consist of health posts, health centers, prefectural hospitals, regional hospitals, and national hospitals. There is a rapid growth of the health private sector in Guinea, providing basic to specialized health services, with very limited or no control by the Ministry of Health. When supported by a program, community health workers (CHWs) attached to health centers provide essential basic care at the community level, particularly in the management and prevention of malaria.

Public health facilities are organized into three levels that provide primary, secondary and tertiary health care. The first level is represented by the health district and consists of three levels:[9]

1. About 925 health posts provide basic primary care and serve several villages (about 3,000 people) each. Health posts are usually staffed by an *agent technique de santé*, a clinical officer with three years of training.

---

[9]The number of health posts and hospitals are based on 2011 estimates; the number of health centers is based on a 2013 estimate.

2.   About 402 health centers provide preventive and curative care and supervise the health posts. Health centers are staffed by several clinicians, including nurses, midwives and doctors.

3.   About 26 district hospitals serve as a reference for health centers and provide care to an average of 285,777 people in the district.

The second level is represented by the regional hospital and serves as a reference for the districts. There are 7 regional hospitals plus 9 municipal hospitals providing care to an estimated 1,401,400 people in the region.

The third level consists of the university hospitals at the national level. This is the highest level of reference for specialized care and includes two such hospitals in the country: Donka and Ignace Deen hospitals, both in Conakry. In addition, there is a highly specialized Sino-Guinean hospital built recently by the Chinese Government.

In addition to public structures, Guinea has a large number of private structures and traditional practitioners. At the community level, CHWs and hygiene committees have the responsibility of understanding health issues, monitoring health programs, and coordinating with local medical officers to improve access and quality of care in their communities.

Access to care is a major problem in Guinea. The MOH estimate that only 55% of the population has access to public health care services. The MOH is investing in community case management through a trained nationwide cadre of CHWs to expand health care access to communities, especially in remote and inaccessible areas. A comprehensive policy on community health care has been elaborated; 3,300 CHWs have been trained and provide health education and basic curative care to surrounding communities – although this has been impacted by the Ebola epidemic, with fewer CHWs providing a standard set of services. The cadre of CHWs has been specifically trained to diagnose malaria using RDTs and provide ACTs to patients with uncomplicated malaria. Guinea's MOH strongly supports integration of priority national health programs, including malaria, HIV/AIDs, neglected tropical diseases, nutrition, reproductive health and family planning, safe delivery, and epidemic surveillance.

4. National malaria control strategy

The national strategic plan covers a period of five years: 2013-2017. The goal is to reduce malaria-related morbidity by 75% from the year 2000, and to reduce malaria mortality to near zero by the end of 2017.

The National Strategic Plan objectives are:

- Protect at least 80% of the population with effective preventive interventions for malaria;
- Ensure biological confirmation of at least 90% of suspected malaria cases;
- Ensure prompt and effective treatment of at least 90% of malaria cases;
- Strengthen monitoring and evaluation (M&E) at all levels in accordance with the NMCP's monitoring and evaluation plan;
- Strengthen management capacity, partnership, and program coordination at all levels; and

- Increase the population's knowledge about prevention and management of malaria.

Main interventions:

- Ensure universal access to prevention measures for the entire population, including ITNs and IPTp;
- Protect the entire population in areas targeted for IRS;
- Ensure laboratory confirmation by RDT or microscopy for all suspected cases of malaria seen in health facilities (public, confessional, and private sectors) and community;
- Ensure proper management of all confirmed malaria cases at all levels of the health pyramid, including the community level;
- Strengthen entomological surveillance in sentinel sites;
- Strengthen epidemiological surveillance of malaria through the Integrated Disease Surveillance and Response system at all levels of the health pyramid;
- Strengthen M&E at all levels for the collection and analysis of high quality data to inform decision making;
- Strengthen behavior change communication (BCC) to increase uptake of malaria prevention and treatment interventions;
- Strengthen coordination capacity and program management at all levels;
- Ensure availability of commodities at all levels for malaria prevention, diagnosis and treatment;
- Strengthen the partnership of Roll Back Malaria (RBM) to mobilize funding through the state budget, the private sector, and partners; and
- Strengthen international and sub-regional cooperation in malaria control.

As described above, the Ebola epidemic has had a devastating impact on the delivery of basic health services and its ability to control malaria. In response to the findings from the Ebola impact survey, the NMCP has developed a strategy to mitigate the impact of the epidemic on malaria prevention and treatment activities. The implementation of this strategy will focus at both the community and the health facility levels.

Community level:

The strategy is based on the WHO recommendations that community health workers should be protected under the principle of universal protection[10].

- Case management: the use of RDTs by the CHW to diagnose malaria is suspended at the community level. The CHW will have to classify suspected malaria cases only on the basic concept of fever or hot body and give appropriate presumptive malaria treatment with artemisinin combination therapy (ACT). This community case management is done without physical contact.

---

[10]World Health Organization. Guidance on temporary malaria control measures in Ebola-affected countries. 2014.

- Communication: Community Health Workers will conduct outreach activities through regular home visits. Awareness activities are to be based on communication materials that will be developed and adapted to the context of the Ebola epidemic. This includes the integration of messages on the prevention of Ebola in interpersonal communication activities, including home visits conducted by the CHWs; educational talks on the prevention of malaria in the context of the Ebola organized for community leaders through community-based organizations in their localities; and mass media and traditional communicators that contribute to community awareness.

To ensure the success of the mitigation strategy, regular consultation between malaria partners and the national Ebola coordination will be necessary.

Health facilities level:

- Case management: The biological confirmation (RDTs or microscopy) of all cases of fever will be systematic in all health facilities with appropriate personal protective equipment (defined as gloves and facial shield to perform an RDT or draw blood). The treatment will be based on national guidelines which includes the use of ACTs for uncomplicated malaria and severe malaria management protocol. In case of persistent of fever after 48 hours, the patient should be referred to an appropriate structure.

- Intermittent Preventive Treatment in Pregnancy: observed treatment (in the presence of medical personnel) should be given with the use of a biodegradable, disposable cup (with potable water) for each pregnant woman.

In all facilities the principle of universal protection must be observed for the protection of both the providers and the public through proper management of biomedical waste. To carry out this strategy, a series of trainings were organized for health providers using a training module adapted to each level.

To ensure proper oversight and follow-up for planned activities, a series of joint (Ministry of Health and partners) supervision visits are planned to be conducted throughout the year with the first one done in March 2015 at all levels, nationwide.

5. Updates in the strategy section

The NMCP has plans to update the national strategy in 2015, mainly due to the Ebola epidemic. However, no concrete timeline has been set for completing this task.

6. Integration, collaboration and coordination

As per the map below, there are two main donors (PMI and Global Fund) that support the malaria program in Guinea. The two donors divide their support across the 8 regions and 33 districts (prefectures) of the country. PMI supports 14 districts in upper and middle Guinea and the 5 communes of Conakry, while Global Fund supports the remaining19 districts in middle Guinea, lower Guinea, and the forest areas. PMI and Global Fund work collaboratively to address the needs that were identified through the gap analysis by NMCP and all its stakeholders. Both donors use the same materials and tools, and collaborate on a number of activities which include: 1) contributing to national needs for malaria commodities; 2) monitoring and evaluation (M&E) using the same M&E tools that support the NMCP such as those used for malaria quarterly reviews, monthly reports, and end-use verification (EUV) surveys; 3) integrated supervision activities conducted jointly with Global Fund and other partners; 4) operations research such as assessing the impact of Ebola on malaria (December 2014); and 5) technical assistance to the NMCP during the preparation of the Global Fund concept note. However, the two donors finance the following activities separately in their own target zones: 1) training and supervision of health care workers and community agents, 2) behavior change communications, and 3) distribution of malaria commodities.

Figure 1. Distribution of PMI and Global Fund Target Zones in Guinea

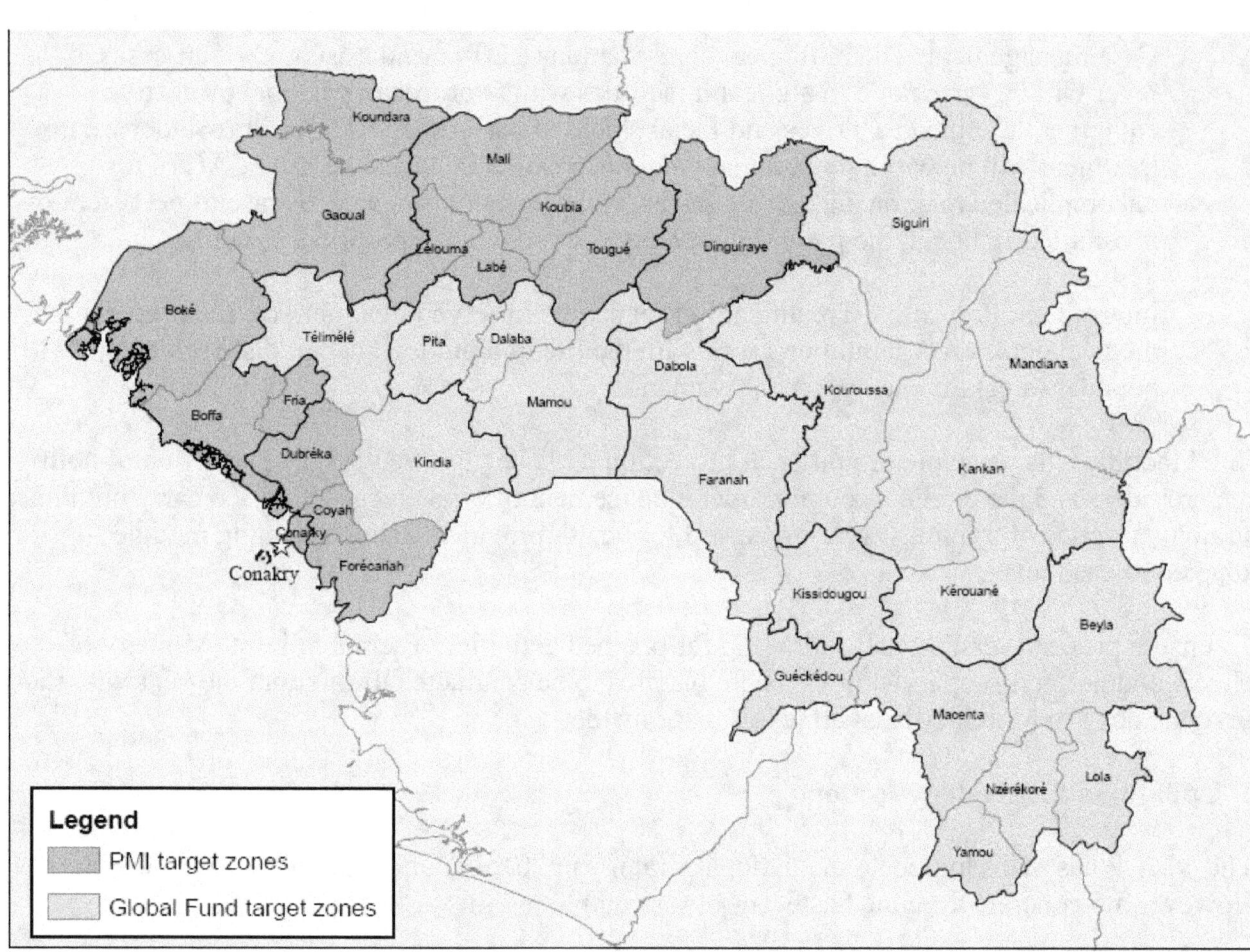

The NMCP has also developed partnerships with other various organizations and institutions involved in the fight against malaria, including Roll Back Malaria (RBM), Research Triangle Institute, Plan Guinea, Population Services International, Catholic Relief Services, German Development Cooperation, *Médecins sans Frontières*, Helen Keller International, Rio Tinto, Islamic Development Bank, World Health Organization (WHO), United Nations Children's Fund (UNICEF), World Bank, and Japanese International Cooperation Agency. This partnership reinforces the collaboration and coordination between malaria stakeholders for the benefit of the Guinean population and will be strengthened by the establishment of a Coordinating Committee of technical and financial partners.

In early 2014, StopPalu implemented a collaborative project with Alcoa, an aluminum mining company operating in Guinea. Under this project, StopPalu organized 7 mobile clinics targeting 12 villages covered by Alcoa activities. Through these activities, 1,304 persons were reached by malaria general information (causes, prevention measures, and treatment methods), 343 persons with fever were tested using RDTs, and 42 persons having positive results received ACT. These activities were conducted by project-trained CHWs, field agents of the project's NGO partners, and project staff under the supervision of the prefecture health team.

In terms of coordination and collaboration of the NMCP with the Ebola response, the NCMP was not well engaged in relevant Ebola response issues - for example, not being informed of new protocols for health providers for symptomatic suspect Ebola cases. Additionally, the health authorities have focused on the Ebola activities to the detriment of other diseases, including malaria, which remains the leading cause of morbidity and mortality in the country.

The NMCP would like to integrate the private and faith-based structures to increase efficiency in the use of available health resources in the country and coordinate the participation of partners in order to reduce malaria mortality and morbidity, particularly among children and pregnant women.

According to the new national strategy, dwindling resources, the involvement of various partners, and the need to rapidly scale up interventions highlight the necessity and urgency of developing mechanisms for integration and effective coordination at national, regional, and district levels.

Strengthening community participation in the planning and delivery of health services to the people is a challenge requiring active involvement of community networks, structured groups, and opinion leaders in all villages.

7. PMI goal, objectives, strategic areas, and key indicators

Under the PMI Strategy 2015-2020, the U.S. Government's goal is to work with PMI-supported countries and partners to further reduce malaria deaths and substantially decrease malaria morbidity, toward the long-term goal of elimination. Building upon the progress to date in PMI-supported countries, PMI will work with NMCPs and partners to accomplish the following objectives by 2020:

1. Reduce malaria mortality by one-third from 2015 levels in PMI-supported countries, achieving a greater than 80% reduction from PMI's original 2000 baseline levels.

2. Reduce malaria morbidity in PMI-supported countries by 40% from 2015 levels.

3. Assist at least five PMI-supported countries to meet the World Health Organization's (WHO) criteria for national or sub-national pre-elimination.[11]

These objectives will be accomplished by emphasizing five core areas of strategic focus:
1. Achieving and sustaining scale of proven interventions
2. Adapting to changing epidemiology and incorporating new tools
3. Improving countries' capacity to collect and use information
4. Mitigating risk against the current malaria control gains
5. Building capacity and health systems towards full country ownership

To track progress toward achieving and sustaining scale of proven interventions (area of strategic focus #1), PMI will continue to track the key indicators recommended by the Roll Back Malaria Monitoring and Evaluation Reference Group (RBM MERG) as listed below:

- Proportion of households with at least one ITN
- Proportion of households with at least one ITN for every two people
- Proportion of children under five years old who slept under an ITN the previous night
- Proportion of pregnant women who slept under an ITN the previous night
- Proportion of households in targeted districts protected by IRS
- Proportion of children under five years old with fever in the last two weeks for whom advice or treatment was sought
- Proportion of children under five with fever in the last two weeks who had a finger or heel stick
- Proportion receiving an ACT among children under five years old with fever in the last two weeks who received any antimalarial drugs
- Proportion of women who received two or more doses of IPTp for malaria during ANC visits during their last pregnancy

8. Progress on coverage/impact indicators to date

Progress in malaria prevention and treatment in Guinea will be assessed by comparing the standardized coverage indicators for ITN ownership and use, IPTp, and prompt and effective treatment across national household surveys. The 2012 DHS provided the first national parasitemia measures. Important progress was shown between the 2005 and 2012 DHS, likely reflecting support from Global Fund Rounds 2 and 6, including a targeted ITN distribution campaign in 2009. In intervening years prior to the 2012 DHS, however, stockouts of ITNs, ACTs, and other commodities slowed initial gains, as reflected in the 2012 DHS results.

According to the 2005 DHS, only 27% of households owned any mosquito net with less than 4% owning an ITN. Only 1% of children under five and pregnant women reported sleeping under an ITN. Less than 3% of women reported receiving at least two doses of SP during their last pregnancy. The 2007 Multiple Indicator Cluster Survey (MICS) showed slight improvements in ITN ownership and use, but these rates were still quite low.

---

[11] http://whqlibdoc.who.int/publications/2007/9789241596084_eng.pdf

The 2009 and 2010 national coverage surveys, conducted with Global Fund financing, appeared to show substantial improvements in key indicators. After a nationwide targeted ITN distribution campaign in 2009, the 2010 survey predictably showed increases in ITN ownership and use: 79% of households reported owning at least one ITN, and 60% of children under five and 47% of pregnant women reported sleeping under an ITN, respectively. Even more striking were the apparent gains in IPTp coverage in 2009 and 2010 compared to the 2005 DHS. While less than 3% of women received two or more doses of SP during their last pregnancy in 2005, 36% and 41% received it in 2009 and 2010, respectively. Direct comparisons between the DHS and the 2009 and 2010 national coverage surveys should be made with caution due to some methodological differences in how indicators were calculated and reported. The specific differences are noted in the indicator table.

The 2012 DHS provided an important data point for ITN coverage since it was conducted prior to the universal coverage campaign implemented in phases from May 2013 through May 2014. Not surprisingly, since over two years had passed since the last targeted distribution (with no routine distribution in the interim) in 2009, ITN coverage and use indicators dropped since the 2010 survey, with less than half of all households reportedly owning an ITN, and 26% and 28% of children under five and pregnant women, respectively, reporting sleeping under an ITN. Coverage of IPTp (at least two doses of SP) also dropped to 18%. The prompt and effective treatment indicator was particularly low with less than 1% of children under five with fever receiving treatment with ACTs within the same or next day of fever onset. Estimates for malaria-associated anemia (cut-off value of Hgb <8g/dl) showed 16% prevalence for children 6-59 months. The country's first parasitemia measures (via microscopy) showed an estimated prevalence of 44% for the country. Conakry had the lowest prevalence at 3%, while the regions with the highest prevalence estimates were Faranah and N'Zérékoré with 66% and 59%, respectively.

Guinea's first Malaria Indicator Survey (MIS) was planned for 2014, but was postponed due to the Ebola epidemic. Amidst community resistance, violence against healthcare workers, and concerns about possible exposure of study teams to Ebola, it was judged to be infeasible to collect biological samples in the community setting. Discussions are currently ongoing regarding the new date for the MIS.

The following table summarizes coverage indicators for malaria control, as well as anemia and parasitemia, from national household surveys since 2005. Due to some variations in survey methodology, specified in the footnotes, not all indicators are directly comparable.

Table I: Evolution of Key Malaria Indicators in Guinea from 2005 to 2012

Malaria Indicator	DHS 2005	MICS 2007	National Coverage Surveys		DHS 2012
			2009	2010	
Percent of households with at least one ITN	3.5%	12.5%	23.4%	78.8%	47.4%
Percent of households with at least one ITN for every two people	-	-	-	-	9.7%
Percent of children under five years old who slept under an ITN the previous night	1.4%	6.7%	12.0%	60.4%	26.1%
Percent of pregnant who slept under an ITN the previous night	1.4%	5.1%	24.7%*	46.8%*	28.3%
Percent of children under five years old with fever in the last two weeks for whom advice or treatment was sought	-	-	-	-	37.1%
Percent of children under five years old with fever in the last two weeks who had a finger or heel stick	-	-	-	-	8.5%
Percent of children receiving an ACT among children under five years old with fever in the last two weeks who received any antimalarial drugs***	-	-	-	-	4.8%
Percent of women who received 2+ doses of IPTp during their last pregnancy in the last 2 years	2.7%	-	35.9%**	41.0%**	17.8%
Percent of children age 6-59 months with severe anemia (Hgb <8g/dl)[12]	14.5%	-	-	-	15.9%
Percent of children age 6-59 months with parasitemia according to microscopy	-	-	-	-	43.9%

The 2009 survey report specifies use of LLINs by pregnant women while the 2010 survey report does not (i.e., it includes any treated nets).

** *The 2009 and 2010 coverage surveys include a five-year look-back period instead of a two-year period and do not specify that at least one dose was taken at an ANC visit.*

*** *ACTs were not the first-line treatment at the time of the DHS and MICS surveys; the 2010 coverage survey report did not provide adequate data to calculate this indicator in the standard format (i.e., the denominator could not be determined).*

---

[12] A measure of hemoglobin <8g/dl is the value typically used as an indirect indicator of anemia associated with malaria.

9. Other relevant evidence on progress

As PMI begins its fifth year of program implementation and benefits from some continuity of operations, it is evident that the country's malaria program has achieved (or is in the process of achieving) some major milestones: the first universal coverage long lasting insecticide-treated net campaign, the implementation of routine distribution of ITNs during ANC and Expanded Program on Immunizations (EPI) visits, decreased stockouts of ACTs, roll out of RDTs, and the first nationally representative parasitemia estimates. In addition, both epidemiological and malaria commodities data in PMI target zones are now flowing from health facilities to the district level to be compiled and sent to the national level.

There is also evidence of increased capacity at the NMCP to coordinate and guide activities throughout the country. New staff has been hired and important processes such as the Malaria Program Review have helped the program take a critical look at its operations and revise its National Strategic Plan, M&E Plan, and policy guidelines, which were signed in early 2014.

A new monthly malaria bulletin was introduced starting October 2014. The two-page bulletin is prepared by the NMCP M&E team from data from monthly reports submitted by health facilities and summarizes key malaria indicators by health district, includes a map showing the malaria incidence by health district during the preceding month, and highlights health facilities reporting high rates of malaria cases.

In parallel, also starting October 2014, the NMCP introduced a new internal, monthly commodity report. This report summarizes commodity data at the district and health facility level, reporting the total stock, the average monthly consumption, and the number of months of stock left for each malaria-related commodity. The monthly commodity reports are used to estimate monthly consumption throughout the country, and to monitor the level of stocks at the district and health facility level to identify areas in risk of stockouts and areas that are over-stocked. However, there is lack of data on previous deliveries of commodities at the decentralized level prior to the initiation of the reporting system.

Local research conducted by the Mafèrinyah Training and Research Center has contributed to the knowledge base of malaria in Guinea:

- A therapeutic efficacy study conducted between 2011 and 2012 in subjects aged six months to 45 years has shown adequate clinical and parasitological response of 97%.[13] This study followed the WHO protocol, including a standard 28-day follow-up period.
- An epidemiological study aimed at examining the seasonal burden of malaria (low and high transmission seasons) in Guinea's four climatic zones is ongoing. Recent discussions with the Mafèrinyah researchers have revealed potential areas for PMI collaboration for operational research and M&E. Mafèrinyah Training and Research Center was chosen to implement the 2015 therapeutic efficacy study in two sites, starting May 2015.

---

[13] Oral communication, *La Société Ivoirienne de Parasitologie et de Mycologie* (SIPAM), conference, Abidjan, 2013.

A new collaboration between the NMCP and the University of Gamal Abdel Nasser of Conakry has resulted in the selection of rooms at the University for the creation of a laboratory and insectary. These will be used for analysis of mosquitoes collected in the entomological sentinel sites and for bioassays on nets collected from the field.

10. Challenges and opportunities

Challenges

The overall lack of healthcare supply in quantity and quality, the unequal distribution between urban and rural areas, the low geographical accessibility and financial assistance to care for the majority of the population are key challenges.

The weakening of the health system due to the Ebola epidemic has affected all malaria interventions and jeopardizes progress to date. Specific challenges include lack of trust and adherence of the population to observe hygiene measures such as hand washing with chlorine, reluctance of parents to get their children immunized, low number of staff in health facilities, difficulty for health workers to make differential diagnosis between malaria and Ebola, lack of communication tools, and threat of rejection of health workers and CHWs by the population.

The NMCP infrastructure is weakened by inadequate material, human, and financial resources:

- The NMCP's capacity for partner coordination, monitoring and evaluation, logistics management and training and supervision is relatively weak due to limited technical capacity, lack of resources, and poor infrastructure, including the NMCP office being located in the middle of a busy market. All of these factors pose challenges to productivity.
- Challenges related to staff training and capacity (and in some cases with unclear terms of reference) prevent the NMCP from performing at full potential given limited resources.
- Lack of finances precludes the NMCP from procuring needed supplies and commodities and meeting operational expenses. As an illustration, only 2.54% (approximately $22 million) of the national budget is allocated to the health sector by the Government of Guinea (GOG). Seventy percent of the annual national budget pays for salaries, leaving only $6 million to purchase vaccines and support management of health facilities.

Limitations to capacity for case management are linked to the following constraints:

- CHWs were not paid for doing malaria case management, so many are no longer continuing malaria work because of the stipend given by the non-governmental organizations (NGOs) working for Ebola. As per PMI policy, CHWs supported by PMI were not given stipends and there is no plan to do so in the future.
- The National Recovery Plan in one of its priority areas is requesting donor support to give retention incentives of 600 USD/year for CHW (i.e., 50 USD/month). In this plan, there is an estimated workforce of 10,000 CHWs nationwide. Although this plan is pending donor response there is an expectation that existing programs will address any

aspects of the plan that fit within their current scopes. To date, partners with existing programs are advocating with the GOG and providing health systems strengthening support to the MOH to enhance its' capacity to recruit, train, retain and pay health workers. While non-monetary incentives alone may have limited appeal in areas where CHWs are being paid for Ebola-related work, non-monetary incentives such as supportive supervision, appropriate job aides, regular replenishment of supplies, badges, awards, training, and educational opportunities remain critical and may have significant appeal in the absence of Ebola as monetary or in-kind incentives are advocated either through the GOG or local communities.

- New WHO recommendations to limit diagnostic testing by CHWs and health workers without effective barrier protection is an increasing concern and will present a significant challenge for malaria case management now and into the future – even when the epidemic is over. At the beginning of the epidemic, health care workers (HCW) stopped using RDTs all together in the forest region. After WHO issued new case management guidelines in November 2014, the NMCP adopted these guidelines only in the Ebola-affected areas, leaving in effect the normal malaria guidelines in the non-affected areas. The NMCP's new malaria guidelines made two scenarios: if appropriate protective equipment is available, HCWs should test suspect malaria cases and treat according to results; in the absence of protective equipment, HCWs should treat presumptively, observe the patient, and refer as needed. In reality, the RDT consumption data suggests low compliance with the new guidelines despite training of HCWs. For the purposes of the MOP, we anticipate that the Ebola epidemic will be over in 2017 and the country will return to pre-Ebola universal testing policy for suspect malaria cases.

- Inadequate M&E and data collection systems (health and logistical information management) limit the NMCP's ability to obtain reliable data on disease burden, service access and utilization, quality and quantity of services provided, and needs, stocks, and consumption of commodities to guide policy and practice, especially in the other 19 districts not supported by PMI.

- Supervision activities are planned to ensure the quality of services, but the cost remains a challenge, especially when there are not many partners who support this activity.

- The supply chain and pharmaceutical system is weak and under reform based on the European Union (EU) audit report recommendations which are implemented at a very slow pace.

Opportunities

As part of the re-building process of the health system, in response to the impact of the Ebola epidemic, several partners such as Japan, France, Brazil, China and Russia, Plan International, *Médecins Sans Frontières* (MSF), International Committee of the Red Cross, ALIMA, Centers for Disease Control and Prevention (CDC), World Bank, UNICEF, World Food Program , UN Mission for Ebola Emergency Response (UNMEER) and Save the Children have recently provided technical and financial support to the Ebola response in the framework of bilateral cooperation. All have announced that they will continue their action on the ground to strengthen the health system.

The development of the short- and medium-term response by the MOH, which fits within the broader national planning process (National Health Development Plan 2015-2024) and with its first phase (2015-2017), is based on the following priorities: zero cases of Ebola and zero deaths; implementation of monitoring mechanisms; detection and response to future epidemics; support for the establishment of a resilient health system at the district level, and improving the governance of the health sector.

There is strong partnership with NMCP and its various partners, having worked together to preserve the efforts and minimize the impact of Ebola on malaria activities. Active engagement of donors and partners represent opportunities for progress in malaria control in Guinea. In addition to the major donors, other partners such as the Islamic Development Bank, Japanese International Cooperation Agency, WHO, UNICEF, World Bank, and local NGOs help the program leverage resources as long as they are fully engaged with the NMCP. The strong potential for collaboration with the Peace Corps includes having volunteers support malaria prevention and education activities. However, at present all Peace Corps volunteers have been evacuated from the country, so restart of this collaboration will likely depend on the end of the epidemic.

Additionally, improved communications with the Maferinyah Training and Research Center has the potential to support improved training and research in Guinea. Although considered symbolic, the contribution of mining companies to malaria control efforts in Guinea is an opportunity that can be better leveraged with stronger coordination and constant dialogue between the government of Guinea and mining operators.

Discussions amongst the NMCP, PMI, and the Global Fund have resulted in an agreement to pursue a new approach for commodity procurement and distribution throughout the country. Rather than divide the country in "target zones," each donor will procure commodities to meet national gaps in coverage and distribute commodities as needed without differentiation between zones. This mechanism helps to mitigate some of the stockout issues that have been a problem in the country.

Furthermore, USAID in its efforts to contribute to the recovery of the health system from the impact of the Ebola epidemic has developed and submitted a malaria proposal that was submitted to USAID/Washington requesting funding to support the revitalization of community case management.

In addition, the approaches used by PMI to promote health seeking behavior and improve access to services align with the strategy in the Health Service Delivery (HSD) Program so the programs will reinforce each other. The efforts to improve referral and integrate services are intended to identify pregnant women and children who fall ill more regularly and ensure that they are provided with the appropriate treatment. The activities to improve supply chain and pharmaceutical management will benefit PMI, and other infectious disease programs, through improving the Central Pharmacy of Guinea (PCG) and the national pharmaceutical supply chain. There will be close coordination with PMI through its implementing partners. In the first quarter the HSD Program will be expected to develop joint activities with PMI's current health services partner specifically to integrate malaria services for pregnant women and children at the facilities levels and through community health workers in malaria high risk areas impacted by Ebola. The Ebola outbreak has had a devastating impact on both reproductive, maternal, newborn and child health (RMNCH) and malaria services, so the HSD Program and PMI will work together to develop and implement activities to support and train community health workers to safely bring services to communities and households as and where appropriate. In response to requests in the Guinean health system revitalization plans for support to human resources for health, USAID and other donors are proposing health system strengthening initiatives that will enhance the capacity of the MOH to hire, train, retain, effectively distribute, incentivize and provide adequate financing for all cadres of health care workers.

III. OPERATIONAL PLAN

1. Insecticide-treated nets

NMCP/PMI objectives

The current objective is to reach 80% coverage of the population at risk of malaria with insecticide treated nets (ITNs) by the end of 2017. The strategy for reaching this objective includes universal campaigns and routine distribution for pregnant women and children less than one year old through antenatal care (ANC) and the Expanded Program on Immunization (EPI). The national strategic plan currently calls for a universal coverage campaign in 2016. The definition of universal coverage adopted by the NCMP is one ITN per two persons.

Progress since PMI was launched

The 2012 Demographic Health Survey (DHS) indicated that 47% of households had at least one ITN. The percentages of those reported as sleeping under an ITN the previous night was 26% for children under the age of five, and 28% for pregnant women. In households with at least one ITN, 51% of children under the age of five and 59% of pregnant women slept under an ITN the previous night. These data were collected between June and October 2012, which was three years after the first distribution of ITNs in 2009 that targeted children under the age of five and pregnant women. The second mass distribution campaign began in May 2013 in Global Fund supported zones and was completed in June 2014. The campaign used a household voucher distribution approach that allowed community members to redeem nets at a designated site on a specific day in their locality. During the first campaign phase (May 2013) over 3.2 million ITNs were distributed in 19 prefectures with over 98% of campaign coupons recovered. Approximately 237,000 PMI-procured nets were used to cover the gap in nets needed in the first campaign phase. After this first phase of distribution, the second phase was the distribution in PMI-targeted zones, which took place in October to November 2013 (14 prefectures) in which 2,061,584 ITNs were distributed. PMI supplied 1,353,000 nets with the remainder provided by other partners (IDB, JICA and UNICEF) to cover the gap in the later phase of the campaign. In addition, reprogrammed FY 2013 funds were used to cover the costs of transporting these ITNs to distribution sites, planning, training, supervision, and social mobilization/communication for the campaign's second phase.

Progress during the last 12-18 months

The third phase of the mass distribution was completed by early June 2014 in the five communes of Conakry, which has the lowest malaria prevalence throughout the country (measured to be 3% during the 2012 DHS). The NMCP originally planned to use the 2014 Malaria Indicator Survey (MIS) to get post-campaign coverage estimates, but this was postponed due to the Ebola epidemic, and a new date has not been determined.

Routine distribution of nets through ANC and EPI facilities started in December 2014 in PMI-supported zones and in March 2015 in Global Fund zones. Prior to the distribution, PMI in collaboration with the NMCP and the Global Fund developed a protocol, generated tools such as vouchers for net distribution and monitoring, and also revised ANC cards. A national quantification exercise estimated the number of ITNs needed, based on expected ANC and EPI attendance. Given that the facility-based distribution coincided with the Ebola epidemic, CDC Foundation helped to fund the initial phase to ensure a successful start of the distribution channel. As of May 2015, a total of 396,845 ITNs were distributed (109,745 by PMI and 287,100 by Global Fund). In June/July 2015, PMI and Global Fund conducted a joint evaluation in the distribution areas to collect information and lessons for the future phases of the distribution. Preliminary results showed that the level of ANC and EPI attendance increased significantly since the distribution began and that there is good provider knowledge on the routine distribution strategy including knowledge on the target groups, messaging, the use of net tracking, and reporting tools. In the areas around Conakry however, the results showed low performance in the completion of tools such as missing information of phone numbers on the vouchers and the ANC cards and incomplete or missing net ordering cards.

Summary of routine ITN distribution

Partner contributions	ITNs procured	ITNs distributed (up to May 2015)	ITNs to be distributed
PMI	180,000	109,745	70,255
Gobal Fund	462,450	287,100	175,350

According to district health reports, the private sector (private associations and nonprofit, faith-based facilities) accounts for about 60% of consultations for primary health care mostly in the city of Conakry. Given the vital role the private sector plays in the health sector and the fact that the country's planning and quantification for malaria commodities has always included this population, the NMCP has embarked on a very intensive plan of action to engage the private sector in the management of malaria, including the distribution of public malaria commodities such as nets and ACTs. The NMCP has developed a memorandum of understanding that will be signed by all private non-profit entities that will be partnering with the program in malaria activities. Orientation sessions with the heads of private entities have taken place and the training of private providers has also been conducted. PMI supported the revision and adaptation of training materials and reporting tools for this purpose. In light of the multi-partner accord (including Global Fund and PMI) whereby all malaria commodities are placed into a common basket and made available throughout the country based on need, PMI is reviewing the possibility and implication of having its commodities distributed through the private sector and will ensure that PMI leadership is in agreement with any revised approaches to ITN distribution, before committing resources. In the memorandum, private entities have committed to follow the national policy and guidelines, undergo routine supervisions and to submit monthly reports to the NMCP about malaria activities.

Commodity gap analysis

Table II. ITN Gap Analysis

ITN Gap Analysis			
Calendar Year	**2015**	**2016**	**2017**
Total targeted population	12,132,795	12,508,912	12,896,688
Routine Distribution Needs			
ANC	464,079	506,612	551,333
EPI	485,312	500,356	515,868
Estimated Total Need for Routine	949,391	1,006,968	1,067,201
Mass Distribution Needs			
2016 universal coverage campaign	0	6,949,396	0
Estimated Total Need for Campaigns	0	6,949,396	0
Total Calculated Need: Routine and Campaign	949,391	7,956,364	1,067,201
Partner Contributions			
PMI	235,000	871,218	600,000
Global Fund	5,210,417	498,776	0
Islamic Development Bank		1,000,000	Unknown
OMVS		600,000	Unknown
Guinea		100,000	Unknown
Estimated Total Partner Contributions	5,445,417	3,069,994	600,000
Total ITNs available in calendar year	5,445,417	7,566,020	600,000
Total ITN Surplus* (Gap)	4,496,026	(390,344)	(467,201)

Surpluses are carried over into the next year, but deficits are not. Assumptions: Pregnant women are 4.5% of the total population. Children under 1 are 4% of the total population. Attendance of pregnant women by ANC (i.e., first visit) is 85% in 2015, 90% in 2016, and 90% in 2017. Children included under EPI equal 100%. The universal campaign need is the total population divided by 1.8.

Plan and justification

With FY 2016 funds, PMI proposes to procure and distribute 600,000 ITNs for routine distribution. PMI will work with the NMCP and partners to improve the routine system to ensure delivery of ITNs to facilities as they need them, as well as support training around a services provided during routine visits.

Proposed activities with FY 2016 funding: ($3,420,000)

1. *Procurement and delivery of ITNs:* Procure 600,000 conical ITNs for routine distribution. This funding will include the cost of the nets and delivery to the district level *($3,060,000)*;
2. *Distribution of ITNs:* Distribute approximately 600,000 ITNs for routine services through the regular primary care package of services including ANC and EPI *($360,000)*; and
3. *BCC for ITN use:* Continue to promote ITN use as part of the integrated communication strategy following national guidelines and in collaboration with other partners *(costs covered in BCC section)*.

2. Indoor residual spraying

NMCP/PMI objectives

The 2013-2017 National Malaria Control Strategy includes indoor residual spraying (IRS) as an intervention area, but it is not currently operationalized and has not been used outside of emergency situations, including use in refugee camps between 2001 and 2005. IRS is also used by some mining companies in limited areas throughout the country. Although IRS is not currently a funded activity within the national strategy for vector control, it is under consideration for future use.

Progress since PMI was launched

In July 2012 PMI funded a ten-day training course for 22 entomology personnel including entomologists from the MOH (four at the NMCP, one at the National Public Health Laboratory, one at the National Directorate of Public Hygiene, and three at the center for research in Maferinyah) and 13 entomological technicians from 7 prefectures. Mosquito surveys and limited insecticide susceptibility assays were carried out in September 2012 in Boffa.

Progress during the last 12-18 months

In the past year, sentinel sites have been identified in all four ecological regions for routine entomological surveillance, which includes pyrethrum spray catches, human landing catches, and light trap collection. In early 2014, entomological collections in Kissidougou and Kankan revealed a predominance of *Anopheles gambiae s.l.* in indoor collections. Both M and S molecular forms of *An. gambiae s.s.* were found in Kankan and Kissidougou, where a high *kdr* frequency was also noted. In addition, insecticide susceptibility tests indicated presence of pyrethroid resistance, but further bioassays will be needed to understand the spread of resistance in Guinea. Results from the insecticide susceptibility testing are included in the table below.

Corrected mortality (and number tested) of *Anopheles gambiae s.l.* tested in WHO susceptibility tests in three sites in Guinea

Site	Deltamethrin 0.05%	Permethrin 0.75%	Alphacypermethrin 0.10%	Lambdacyhalothrin 0.05%	DDT 4%	Bendiocarb 0.10%
Boke	86 (45)	88 (42)	-	-	44 (45)	100 (45)
Kissidougou	100 (42)	18 (40)	58 (40)	61 (43)	28 (44)	87 (40)
Faranah	100 (75)	43 (75)	-	-	31 (75)	100 (75)

Although no IRS activities are currently underway, the resistance status of malaria vectors is important for understanding the role of resistance in relation to the use of ITNs. It will also provide useful information if IRS is undertaken in the future. Development of an insecticide resistance management plan will be another important area of focus in the coming year.

An agreement has been reached with the *Université de Conakry Gamal Abdel Nasser* to use rooms therein for a laboratory and insectary. The refurbishment of the rooms is underway.

In January 2015, three staff members from the vector control division of the NMCP were sent for a two-month training at the *Centre de Recherche Entomologique de Cotonou* (CREC) in Benin. The training will prepare these staff for the laboratory work needed to analyze mosquitoes collected in the sentinel site collections.

Plan and justification

The plan for FY 2016 funding is the continued collection of entomological data from sentinel sites that began in January 2014. These data will provide information on the species of malaria vectors, infection rates, biting times, and resistance status. Furthermore, the collection of data at three times during the year will allow for estimation of seasonal effects.

Proposed activities with FY 2016 funding: ($354,000)

1. *Entomological monitoring and capacity building:* Support for surveillance of vectors and insecticide resistance in each of the four ecological zones; establishment of a permanent insectary and laboratory including procurement of equipment and supplies, capacity building for entomologists, and resources for insectary operations; ITN durability monitoring; and support for NMCP staff (per diems, etc.), *($285,000)*;
2. *Advanced training of entomological technicians*: Four regional technicians based in the sentinel sites will be trained at the *Centre Muraz* in Bobo-Dioulasso to allow collections of mosquitoes and insecticide resistance tests to be done with reduced supervision from the NMCP *($40,000)*; and
3. *Technical assistance for entomological capacity building:* Support for two technical assistance visits from CDC to continue assistance to develop entomological capacity *($29,000)*.

3. Malaria in pregnancy

NMCP/PMI objectives

In 2013, the NMCP presented their new strategy (2013-2017) with a revised version adopted in February 2014. The NMCP and the National Safe Motherhood Program (which oversees ANC services nationwide) worked together to develop the national malaria strategy and protocols. The strategy contains guidance on standard WHO recommended practices for the prevention of malaria in pregnancy including the administration of IPTp with SP under the direct observation of an ANC attendant, at four-week intervals, starting in the second trimester (from week 13), with at least three treatments given before delivery, and the provision of an ITN at the time of the first visit. Iron/folate is provided free of charge at ANC. Each pregnant woman receives 30 tablets (60mg/0.25mg per tablet) per month, taking one per day. Regarding case management of malaria in pregnancy (MIP), pregnant women who are diagnosed with uncomplicated malaria should receive quinine in the first trimester and an ACT in the second and third trimesters. Treatment for those diagnosed with severe malaria follow national protocols (see section on Treatment). The strategy also follows WHO guidance regarding pregnant women who are HIV positive.

CHWs conduct home visits to encourage pregnant women to attend ANC to receive IPTp (among other things), and to use nets every night to protect themselves from malaria. There are no data available on the number of CHW interactions with pregnant women. Moreover, though numbers have started to pick up, in the current context of Ebola both facility attendance and CHW interaction with the community has dropped off significantly.

According to the national strategy, pregnant women represent an estimated 4.5% of the population, which is the percentage that the NMCP uses to quantify needs for SP and routine ITN distribution through ANC.

The NMCP target is that by the end of 2015, 85% of pregnant women will have received at least three SP treatments (IPTp3). By 2016, the target will be 90%, and will remain the same in 2017. The national strategy defines a target of 80% ITN use by pregnant women (same target in all years). In addition, by the end of 2015, 70% of pregnant women will receive an ITN during an ANC visit, which increases to 100% in 2016 and beyond. PMI will work with the NMCP and partners to achieve progress towards IPTp uptake and ITN distribution targets.

Progress since PMI was launched

Since the launch of PMI in Guinea in FY 2011, PMI assisted the NMCP to revise its national strategy to reflect current WHO recommendations for IPTp uptake. Also, PMI procured and distributed nationwide over 1 million SP treatments; trained over 1,600 health facility workers (exceeding the FY 2014 target of 1,536 health facility workers) and over 700 CHWs (exceeding the FY 2014 target of 680 CHWs) in MIP as part of integrated refresher training courses; and reached over 200,000 people via home visits and community-level activities such as group discussions. The trainers for MIP are from the National Safe Motherhood Program and work with trainers from the NMCP and other MOH units to form the core, integrated training team that PMI has been supporting for all training. Communication messages were disseminated throughout PMI target zones promoting IPTp uptake at ANC and sleeping under ITNs every night (see BCC section for more details).

The data from the 2012 DHS show that while 85% of pregnant women make at least one ANC visit, only 18% receive two or more doses of IPTp (up from 3% in the 2005 DHS). DHS data also show that 28% of pregnant women slept under an ITN the previous night, up from 1.4% in the 2005 DHS. It should be noted that implementation of IPTp was hampered by stockouts of SP for the first two years of PMI in Guinea. Also, ITNs have only begun appearing in ANCs over the past year, so the indicator from the DHS may be a reflection of the ITNs that were distributed nationwide for vulnerable groups in 2009, including women of reproductive age and children under five years of age. There is concern that the Ebola epidemic will have a negative impact on all indicators linked to health service delivery, including ANC, so expectations are modest, in spite of increased availability of SP and ITNs in ANCs.

Progress during the last 12-18 months

During the last 12 months PMI procured 375,000 SP treatments. This consignment was made available for nationwide distribution. The plan moving forward will be for PMI to procure and distribute SP for the entire country, starting in 2015.

Over the past year, 180,000 nets were delivered to clinics, and an additional 235,000 ITNs have arrived in country to support the routine distribution of ITNs through ANC. These contributions will cover almost 50% of the need for routine nets for pregnant women. ITNs are also on order from the Global Fund and should fill the remaining gap in the country.

PMI also provided support for training and supervision of ANC workers in IPTp and for the dissemination of communication messages to increase knowledge and promote MIP prevention at the community level. Training materials have been updated and are following the new guidelines for IPTp.

Across PMI target zones, about 3,810 health facility workers and 1,329 CHWs were trained on malaria case management; health workers were trained on MIP as well. There are 9,764 health workers and approximately 4,100 CHWs nationwide. Thus, over the past 18 months, PMI trained 39% and 32% respectively of all health workers and CHWs nationwide. The training was done based on new case management guidelines issued by the MOH in the context of Ebola. It should be noted that even though training has taken place and commodities are being provided, there is evidence of a considerable decline in public health facility attendance, in combination with health worker attrition and health facility closures.

Commodity gap analysis

With a national population of approximately 12 million, and the proportion of pregnant women estimated at 4.5%, it is projected that 580,351 pregnancies could occur in 2017. PMI will procure approximately 1,565,000 treatments of SP to meet 100% of the nationwide need (90% of all pregnant women). Starting in 2015, the NMCP has requested that PMI be responsible for all SP purchases nationwide. One important caveat to this analysis is that the long-term impact of Ebola on health service delivery is not yet known. SP projections were made in the gap analysis prior to Ebola for the purpose of the Global Fund concept note submission by the NMCP, and represent the targets set by the NMCP. As of 2015, health facility attendance, including ANC has dropped off considerably, particularly in Ebola-affected areas. In response, there will be close and careful monitoring of stocks to better forecast and order replacement supplies of all commodities, including SP. The NMCP and its partners are reviewing pre-Ebola quantifications to make the necessary adjustments, delaying filling and shipping orders for commodities, including SP, when appropriate. If the Ebola crisis continues, or facility attendance remains low, the team will work with the National Malaria Control Officer to consider reprogramming these funds next year. Currently, the NMCP is hesitant to drop all orders or drastically change forecasted commodity needs as they recognize the length of time required to fill orders and get them into the country. They do not want to experience massive stockouts, which were the norm prior to PMI's arrival in 2011.

Table III. SP Gap Analysis for Malaria in Pregnancy

Calendar Year	2015	2016	2017
Total population	12,132,795	12,508,912	12,896,688
SP Needs			
Total number of pregnant women attending ANC	464,079	506,611	580,351
Total SP Need (in treatments)	1,392,238	1,519,833	1,565,000
Partner Contributions			
SP carried over (deficit) from previous year	0	0	0
SP from MOH	0	0	0
SP from Global Fund	771,248	597,370	0
SP from other donors	0	0	0
SP planned with PMI funding	620,990	922,463	1,565,000
Total SP Available	1,392,238	1,519,833	1,565,000
Total SP Surplus (Gap)	0	0	0

Assumptions: Population growth is estimated at 3.1% and based on 2009 population data. Pregnant women are estimated to be approximately 4.5% of the population. Target for ANC attendance (i.e., IPTp 3) is 85% in 2015 and 90% in 2016 and 2017. The NMCP bases SP needs on 3 doses for each pregnant woman attending ANC.

Plan and justification

PMI will continue to support activities aimed at enhancing the provision of effective MIP services in public health facilities in Guinea. PMI will procure enough SP treatments to cover 100% of the estimated needs nationwide (based on 90% attendance at ANC), as well as a portion of the ITN need for routine distribution during ANC visits (see ITN section). Given the tremendous drop off in health facility attendance due to the Ebola epidemic, PMI will continue to support BCC training and messaging to reinvigorate the demand for ANC services.. Additionally, PMI will support laboratory diagnosis and appropriate treatment of malaria to reinforce the implementation of MIP services, including training and supervision of IPTp service delivery along with other aspects of effective case management, and promotion of ITN use.

Proposed activities with FY 2016 funding: ($193,000)

1. _Treatments of SP:_ Procure approximately 1,565,000 treatments of SP to cover 100% of the needs in Guinea for 2017_($187,000)_;
2. _Supplies to ensure consumption of SP at ANC:_ Procure supplies such as cups and water to ensure that SP is taken at the time of ANC visit _($6,000)_;
3. _Promote BCC for IPTp_: Promote ANC clinic attendance and educate pregnant women and communities on the benefits of IPTp. This activity will include support for community-level approaches, such as training of community-based workers, as well as mass media (including local radio stations). Immunization outreach sessions will be used as opportunities for educating women. This will be part of a larger integrated BCC activity to satisfy needs for case management, ITNs, and IPTp _(Costs covered in BCC section)_;
4. _Training/refresher training for MIP_: Provide training and refresher training for public and private health facility midwives and nurses to correctly deliver SP in the context of the focused ANC approach. Training will include benchmark assessments, on-the-job training of the current treatment algorithm, and coaching. Training will be part of an integrated training package _(Costs covered in Case Management/Diagnosis section)_; and
5. _Supervise health workers in IPTp to improve quality of service:_ Provide on-site supervision for public health facility midwives and nurses to correctly deliver SP in the context of the focused ANC approach, and to ensure that available ITNs are given to women at their first ANC contact. Supervision will continue to be part of an integrated approach for supervision at health facilities, including ANC, immunization, and case management services with appropriate rooms and relevant staff supervised. _(Costs covered in Case Management/Diagnosis section)_.

4. Case management

a. Diagnosis and Treatment

NMCP/PMI objectives

Prior to the scale-up of rapid diagnostic test (RDT) availability, national malaria case management guidelines allowed for clinical diagnosis of malaria. However, with increasing RDT availability, PMI supported the revision of the NMCP guidelines to reflect WHO recommendations on laboratory confirmation of all suspect malaria cases prior to treatment. According to NMCP policy, laboratory confirmation of cases could be done either by RDTs, provided free of charge and widely used at public health facilities and by CHWs, or by microscopy, a paid service at health facilities. This requirement applies to both forms of malaria (uncomplicated and severe) and at all levels of the health system, including the community level.

Diagnosis

According to Guinea's health services package, all hospitals and health centers should provide microscopy services. However, a Global Fund-financed health facility survey of hospitals and health centers in 2010 showed that fewer than half the facilities in Guinea had a microscope (approximately 100% of hospitals but only 40% of health centers).[14] Microscopes often are not functional and health facilities may lack reagents and related laboratory supplies. Data from the health facility survey indicated that only 43% of hospitals and health centers had slides, and 19% had Giemsa stain. Staff from the NMCP and the National Laboratory, which is part of the National Institute of Public Health, are responsible for supervision of microscopy, although no comprehensive quality assurance/quality control program has been developed for malaria. PMI intends to begin working on this in the future, as the scale-up in training and provision of diagnostic materials moves toward nationwide coverage.

Given the limitations of microscopy services in Guinea, the NMCP supported the introduction of RDTs for malaria diagnosis at all levels of the health care system. In addition to ensuring RDT availability in health facilities, the NMCP also aimed for continuous supply of RDTs at the community level for use by CHWs.

Treatment

In Guinea, the first-line ACTs for treatment of uncomplicated malaria are artesunate-amodiaquine (AS-AQ) and artemether-lumefantrine (AL). In cases of AS-AQ or AL intolerance, side effects, or treatment failure, the patient should be referred to the nearest health facility. Per national policy, pregnant women in their first trimester with uncomplicated malaria are to be treated with oral quinine; in the second and third trimesters, they are to be treated with AS-AQ (or AL). The ACTs are free for adults and children (as are RDTs), but patients have to pay for other drugs received such as paracetemol (systematically prescribed), as well as for microscopy tests.

As stated in the national strategy, the first choice for treatment of severe malaria is injectable artesunate. Other acceptable treatments include injectable artemether or quinine. The management of severe malaria should be carried out in health facilities with the capacity required for proper treatment. All cases of severe malaria in pregnant women should be treated with parenteral quinine during the first trimester of pregnancy, and intramuscular injection of artemisinin derivatives or parenteral quinine from the second trimester onward. Per national policy, treatment for severe malaria is free.

---

[14]This was a nationally-representative survey with a sample of 129 health facilities.

The national case management strategy for CHWs includes the use of RDTs, recognition of danger signs of severe malaria, and pre-referral treatment (with rectal artesunate) of identified severe cases. All cases of severe malaria seen in the community or at health facilities without the capacity to treat severe cases, should receive pre-referral treatment with artemisinin derivatives (intramuscularly or suppository) before referral. Pre-referral treatment is a relatively new intervention and prior to its early-2014 adoption as a national policy, the use of rectal artesunate by CHWs was piloted by *Médecins sans Frontières* Switzerland for three years in the forest region in Gueckedou. Rectal artesunate has been added to the list of drugs that CHWs are permitted to use and it is now part of CHW routine training. Appropriate case management tools, including algorithms, protocols, IEC material, and necessary commodities will be provided to CHWs and they will be supervised by health facility staff. The CHWs do not receive stipends under government policy and PMI will not support providing stipends if circumstances change.

Training

All health providers are to be trained in the diagnosis and treatment of uncomplicated and severe malaria cases. Nationwide there are about 108 laboratory technicians, 9,674 health facility workers, and 4,100 CHWs (approximately 10 per health center). The goal is to eventually train all in RDT use and overall case management. Training will be based on the revised and recently distributed training manuals for health providers on case management and malaria in pregnancy, which includes new algorithms for case management. This refers to pre-Ebola manuals and guidance; additional details on the impact of Ebola on case management are below. Health workers, including CHWs, will be retrained every two years on appropriate case management, including for pre-referral of severe cases, and supervised regularly according to the national supervision strategy.

Supervision

A national supervision plan exists, but a resource gap limits the NMCP's as well as the regional (Regional Health Directorate [DRS]) and district (Prefectural Health Directorate [DPS]) health authorities' ability to conduct effective, comprehensive, and regular supervision. Supervision is planned based on a specific guidance document and focuses on case management and data quality. The following is a description of the national plan (for which resources are not sufficient):

- Central/National level to regional (DRS) levels – Activities at the national level are led by the NMCP and supported by implementing partners – PMI's malaria bilateral and Catholic Relief Services (Global Fund principal recipient). Supervision is scheduled to occur every six months to eight DRS.
- Regional (DRS) to district (DPS) levels – Supervision is organized by DRS and is done with implementing partners. Each DRS typically has 3-6 DPS. Supervision is scheduled to occur every 3 months to 38 DPS.
- District (DPS) to health facilities (925 health posts, 412 health centers, 6 commune health centers, 26 prefecture hospitals, 7 regional hospitals, 3 national hospitals) – Supervision of health facilities is done by DPS and implementing partners. Supervision is scheduled to occur every two months.

Ebola context

The West Africa Ebola epidemic, which began in Guinea in December 2013, has greatly impacted case management in Guinea, driven partly by the overlap between Ebola virus disease and malaria symptoms. Amidst concerns of possible healthcare worker exposure to Ebola during blood draws for malaria laboratory confirmation, the WHO released new recommendations for malaria testing and treatment in Ebola-affected zones.[15] The guidelines recommend suspension of all RDT testing at the community level, and suspension of RDT and microscopy testing at health facilities without appropriate personal protective equipment. Instead, in these settings, all fever cases should be treated presumptively with artemisinin-based combination therapy (ACT). All patients not responding appropriately to treatment with ACTs within 48 hours should be evaluated for possible Ebola virus disease.

The NMCP adopted these temporary guidelines in December 2014, creating a new testing and treatment algorithm for use in Ebola-affected zones. However, even prior to the adoption of the algorithm, malaria diagnosis practices had already changed in Guinea due to the Ebola epidemic. The December 2014 health facility survey found that while laboratory confirmation rates had dramatically gone up between 2013 and 2014 in prefectures not affected by Ebola, they did not significantly change from 2013 to 2014 in prefectures affected by Ebola, despite increasing RDT availability. Moreover, RDT use by CHWs decreased in prefectures affected by Ebola, with only 30% of CHWs reporting using RDTs since the start of the Ebola epidemic compared to 70% prior to the start of the epidemic. For the purposes of the MOP, we anticipate that the Ebola epidemic will be over in 2017 and the country will return to the pre-Ebola universal testing policy for suspect malaria cases with appropriate treatment according to test results. Programming will be adjusted based on the evolution of this health crisis.

Progress since PMI was launched

When PMI started in 2011 the country was completely stocked out of RDTs and there were almost no functioning microscopes anywhere in the country. Since then, PMI has purchased and distributed over 5 million RDTs and purchased 48 microscopes and related supplies (reagents, gloves, disposal boxes, and slides). This will be combined with efforts from Global Fund to make available 100 microscopes: 63 from PMI and 37 from Global Fund. This will ensure that each of the 36 hospitals, nationwide, as well as about 28 health centers will be fully equipped: two microscopes per hospital, and one microscope in each of 28 selected health centers.

PMI has also supported supervision of RDT use at both the health facility and community levels (more recently). Eighteen laboratory technicians have been recruited and trained to serve as supervisors for the Outreach Training and Support Supervision program. Training and supervision activities in diagnostics recently started in the Global Fund zones.

PMI supported the initial update of the national malaria strategy and policy, which included important revisions on the use of diagnostics to confirm suspected malaria cases before treatment, following WHO recommendations. Previously, the strategy and policy did not require

---

[15]World Health Organization. Guidance on temporary malaria control measures in Ebola-affected countries. 2014.

biologic confirmation of malaria in order to prescribe treatment for children less than five years of age.

Building on a PMI-supported rapid laboratory assessment, in March 2012 PMI supported the evaluation of an additional 19 zonal health facilities and found that some facilities did not have a functional microscope, and of the ones that did, all the microscopes were in poor condition. The assessment findings were used to inform activities including a nationwide training of 25 trainers of laboratory technicians in malaria diagnosis, microscopy maintenance, supply management, and RDT use. Additionally, 680 CHWs were trained in RDT use.

Finally, PMI supported the development of an RDT utilization sheet to help CHWs track RDT use and better determine when they should request stock replenishment. PMI also supported training on quantification in PMI target zones so that health facility personnel and regional warehouse managers understand the process and have the tools for calculating supply needs based on use.

With respect to treatment, PMI has provided ACT treatments for all age groups in response to stockouts in health facilities in both PMI and Global Fund zones. PMI procured and distributed injectable quinine and injectable artesunate for the treatment of severe cases. PMI also developed a data collection form, which allowed for a better quantification of needs at the facility level. Commodity distributions have served as an opportunity to introduce the new monthly malaria reporting template and process. Other key activities supported by PMI have included the introduction of a new medication (injectable artesunate) for the treatment of severe malaria and case management training of 3,810 health workers and 1,329 CHWs. There are a total of 9,674 health workers and approximately 4,100 CHWs in total, nationwide.

Table IV: Case management training targets and activities

Training Summary	Project Target	Trained previously by partners (PMI launch-Apr 2013)	Year 1 (Remainder of FY 2013)	Year 2 (FY 2014)	Year 3 (Q1 of FY 2015)
Health facility workers trained in RDTs and case management	856	147	0	1,675	2,135
CHWs trained in RDTs and case management	680	308	0	680	649*
Lab staff trained in microscopy and RDTs	60	64	0	25	0

* Trained on new malaria case management guidelines in context of Ebola epidemic

Progress during the last 12-18 months

In the last year, PMI has procured approximately 2 million ACTs for uncomplicated malaria and 70,000 treatments of injectable artesunate for severe malaria cases. PMI also trained 995 healthcare workers and 680 CHWs in malaria case management. PMI has continued to support supervision of health workers for case management at the hospital, health center, and health post levels, as well as CHWs at the community level. The last EUV, conducted in December 2014, found that over 70% of health centers surveyed had received supervision on case management or drug management in the previous six months, compared to only 43% of hospitals. PMI supported the development of a checklist for supervision, to be utilized as part of an integrated supervision visit, ensuring that malaria diagnostics are performed correctly along with other health worker functions. PMI helped sponsor monthly meetings at the DPS and DRS levels, with focus on malaria case management and data quality.

PMI and partners, including the NMCP, have introduced monthly reporting forms and tools to ensure a more consistent flow of information from the health facility to the district level and up to the central level. This approach has begun in PMI zones and has helped improve completion of monthly reporting to the NMCP from 30% to over 80% in these facilities. After sending monthly reports detailing the number of medicines given to patients, health facilities are re-supplied with malaria products. This approach is still fairly new in the Global Fund zones and the hope is that the data will allow the NMCP and MOH to plan for appropriate procurement and distribution of products to the local level.

The malaria monthly report form was derived from the original Health Management Information System (HMIS) tool. Malaria reporting has improved in term of completeness and timeliness mostly in PMI zones and it is getting better in Global Fund zones. However, overall data quality, completeness, timeliness and accuracy need improvement as well as a more comprehensive integration of malaria, TB, HIV/AIDS, EPI and other priority disease control health information systems into the HMIS. The Ebola epidemic negatively impacted the HMIS, and resulted in its existing workforce migrating to the National Ebola Coordination; it also resulted in highlighting more chronic issues related to personnel, financial support, and operational performance and a coordinated effort on the part of donors to collectively advocate for key changes and better coordinate technical and financial support. (Additional details in the M&E section.)

In addition to commodities stock data, the Guinea EUV collects limited case management data though register review. The December 2014 (most recent) survey found that malaria accounted for 37% of total patient records examined; of these 38% were in children under five years. Of all fever cases recorded, 72% were diagnosed as malaria (including clinical and confirmed cases). Of diagnosed malaria cases in children under five years (clinical and confirmed), 75% were treated with an ACT.

PMI helped support 15 national trainers who were trained on malaria diagnosis. Concurrently, 74 hospital lab technicians were trained on malaria diagnosis (RDT and microscopy). A total of 1,329 CHWs (32% of all CHWs nationwide) were trained or received refresher training on community case management, including on ACT use, RDT use, and recording and reporting of malaria cases using data collection tools. At health facilities, including both public and private facilities, 3,810 healthcare (39% of all health workers nationwide) staff were trained on updated case management protocols and training curricula.

Upon the release of the new WHO guidelines for malaria case management in Ebola-affected zones, PMI supported the adaptation of the existing NMCP malaria guidelines to conform to the new, Ebola-specific guidelines. This included the creation of a new treatment algorithm, which incorporates presumptive treatment of fever cases by CHWs and healthcare workers in health facilities without appropriate personal protective equipment. The new treatment guidelines were introduced in December 2014, and PMI supported the training of CHWs on the new treatment guidelines.

Commodity gap analysis

The table below presents RDT needs and expected partner contributions for 2015, 2016 and 2017, as specified by the gap analysis conducted by the NMCP.

Table V: RDT Gap Analysis

Calendar Year	2015	2016	2017
RDT Needs			
Target population at risk for malaria[a]	12,132,795	12,508,912	12,896,688
Total number projected fever cases[b]	12,132,795	11,258,021	9,027,682
Percent of fever cases confirmed with microscopy[c]	12.0%	13.5%	18.0%
Percent of fever cases confirmed with RDT[c]	68.0%	76.5%	72.0%
Total RDT Needs	**8,250,301**	**8,612,386**	**6,499,931**
Partner Contributions			
RDTs carried over (deficit) from previous year	0	0	0
RDTs from MOH	0	0	0
RDTs from Global Fund	1,888,000	4,112,386	1,999,931
RDTs from other donors	0	0	0
RDTs planned with PMI funding	5,250,000	3,460,000	4,155,000
Total RDTs Available	**7,138,000**	**7,572,386**	**6,154,931**
Total RDT Surplus (Gap)	**(1,112,301)**	**(1,040,000)**	**(345,000)**

[a] *Population growth is estimated at 3.1% and based on 2009 population data.*
[b] *Assuming 1 febrile episode per year per person in 2015, decreasing to 0.9 in 2016 and 0.7 in 2017 to adjust for expected decreases of febrile episodes due to the success of vector-control interventions.*
[c] *Assuming an 80% confirmation rate in 2015, increasing to 90% in 2016 and 2017*

The table below presents ACT needs and expected partner contributions for 2015, 2016 and 2017, as specified by the gap analysis conducted by the NMCP.

Table VI: ACT Gap Analysis

Calendar Year	2015	2016	2017
ACT Needs			
Target population at risk for malaria	12,132,795	12,508,912	12,896,688
Total projected number of malaria cases	5,047,243	4,401,886	3,737,460
Total ACT Needs	**5,047,243**	**4,401,886**	**3,737,460**
Partner Contributions			
ACTs carried over (deficit) from previous year	0	0	0
ACTs from MOH	0	0	0
ACTs from Global Fund	1,136,848	2,401,886	1,737,460
ACTs from other donors	0	0	0
ACTs planned with PMI funding	2,000,000	1,735,000	2,000,000
Total ACTs Available	3,136,848	4,136,886	3,737,460
Total ACT Surplus (Gap)	(1,910,395)	(265,000)	0

Assumptions: Population growth is estimated at 3.1% and based on 2009 population data. The total ACT need is based on the number of expected suspect cases and adjusted for testing rate (80% in 2015, 90% in 2016 and 2017), test positivity rate (52% in 2015, 43% in 2016, and 46% in 2017), and presumptive treatment of cases (20% in 2015, 10% in 2016, and 10% in 2017). The total is adjusted for access to care (assumed to be 100%) and provision of care per the national strategic plan, as well as the expected reduction in expected malaria cases due to the success of vector control strategies (15% in 2016 and 30% in 2017 over 2015 levels).

The table below presents injectable artesunate needs for 2015, 2016 and 2017, as specified by the malaria programmatic gap analysis for 2015 conducted by the NMCP.

Table VII: Injectable Artesunate Gap Analysis

Calendar Year	2015	2016	2017
Severe Malaria Treatment Needs			
Target population at risk for malaria	12,132,795	12,508,912	12,896,688
Total projected number of severe malaria cases	315,453	155,361	83,055
Total Injectable Artesunate Needs	**201,890**	**105,645**	**59,799**
Total Injectable Artemether Needs	**50,472**	**26,411**	**14,950**
Partner Contributions			
Injectable artesunate carried over from previous year	0	82,145	98,762
Injectable artemether carried over from previous year	0	0	5,000
Injectable artesunate from MOH	0	0	0
Injectable artemether from MOH	0	0	0
Injectable artesunate from Global Fund	178,035	46,162	59,799
Injectable artemether from Global Fund	20,654	11,411	14,950
Injectable artesunate from other donors	0	0	0
Injectable artemether from other donors	0	0	0

Calendar Year	2015	2016	2017
Injectable artesunate planned with PMI funding	106,000	76,100	0
Injectable artemether planned with PMI funding	27,200	20,000	0
Total Injectable Artesunate Available	284,035	204,407	158,561
Total Injectable Artemether Available	47,854	31,411	14,950
Total Injectable Artesunate Surplus (Gap)	82,145	98,762	98,762
Total Injectable Artemether Surplus (Gap)	(2,618)	5,000	0

Assumptions: Population growth is estimated at 3.1% and based on 2009 population data. Of all malaria cases (number confirmed plus presumptively treated), 6.3% are expected to be severe in 2015, 3.5% in 2016, and 2.2% in 2017. The total is adjusted for access to care (assumed to be 100%) and provision of care per the national strategic plan. Of severe cases needing treatment, 80% will be treated with injectable artesunate and 20% will be treated with injectable artemether.

The table below presents artesunate suppository needs for 2015, 2016 and 2017, as specified by the malaria programmatic gap analysis for 2015 conducted by the NMCP.

Table VIII: Artesunate Suppository Gap Analysis

Calendar Year	2015	2016	2017
Artesunate Suppository Needs			
Target population at risk for malaria	12,132,795	12,508,912	12,896,688
Total projected number of referred severe malaria cases	11,182	8,747	7,394
Total Artesunate Suppository Needs	**11,182**	**8,747**	**7,394**
Partner Contributions			
Artesunate suppository carried over (deficit) from previous year	0	3,960	10,749
Artesunate suppository from MOH	0	0	0
Artesunate suppository from Global Fund	0	0	0
Artesunate suppository from other donors	0	0	0
Artesunate suppository planned with PMI funding	15,142	15,536	0
Total Artesunate Suppository Available	15,142	19,496	10,749
Total Artesunate Suppository Surplus (Gap)	3,960	10,749	3,355

Assumptions: Population growth is estimated at 3.1% and based on 2009 population data. Assumptions for the total artesunate suppository needs are based on the number of suspect malaria cases expected to seek care at the community level (8% in 2015, 10% in 2016 and 2017). Of these, 3% are assumed to be severe cases needing pre-referral treatment and 100% of those in need are expected to get pre-referral treatment.

Plan and justification

PMI will continue to support the NMCP's national policy of malaria case management based on diagnostic confirmation by supporting RDT use and strengthening microscopy through provision of commodities, as well as training and supervision at the health facility and community levels. PMI supports the entire country with commodity procurement to meet existing needs rather than differentiating between zones. This will reduce stockouts of commodities and increase access to treatment. However, in light of current information on oversupply of case management commodities due to non-use by health facilities, which are functioning at reduced levels (or closed in some circumstances), PMI will continue to closely monitor supplies and make adjustments as needed to ensure that commodities do not expire. The NMCP requested that PMI procure the majority of the country's diagnostics commodities and PMI will continue to procure ACTs for all age groups. To facilitate the distribution of commodities, PMI will procure and deliver to the lowest level necessary to ensure they reach beneficiaries.

Although PMI was not planning to support seasonal malaria chemoprevention (SMC) in Guinea, NMCP, with support from the Malaria Consortium and UNITAID and Catholic Relief Services (CRS), decided to implement SMC in 2015 using amodiaquine plus sulfadoxine-pyrimethamine (AQ+SP) in 6 prefectures located in PMI supported zones. As a result, PMI at the request of NMCP is working with its partners to retrieve all (AQ+SP) from health facilities in these prefectures to return it to PCG and replace it with artemether/lumefantrine (A/L) at least one month before SMC is due to start. In addition, PMI will procure AL for the six SMC districts (total population: 2,268,104) and ASAQ for the remaining districts, and PMI partners will also train health workers on how to prescribe A/L. All severe malaria treatments (injectable artesunate, injectable artemether) that are needed for 2016 will be procured by the Global Fund. No rectal artesunate will be purchased with FY 2016 funds, as the gap analysis suggests that existing stocks to be bought in 2015 and 2016 will be enough to cover needs in 2017.

Training and supervision will continue to provide long-term, ongoing support to strengthen diagnostic services at all levels of the health care system by identifying areas that require improvement and providing on-site feedback and technical advice and support to the front-line clinicians and laboratory staff in peripheral health facilities. Training and supervision for diagnostics will be integrated with community case management as well as other malaria prevention and care activities, and will focus on PMI intervention zones as Global Fund provides support for training and supervision in their designated zones. An estimated 2,200 health workers (including community level) will be targeted for training and supervision in PMI focus areas. One specific component of diagnostic strengthening will be investment in the development of a comprehensive quality assurance and quality control system for microscopy and RDTs. This will ensure sustainable gains and country capacity building in diagnostic practices.

PMI plans to support integrated BCC activities to promote appropriate treatment-seeking behavior among community members. Human capacity building will continue to be a part of this intervention through clinical and refresher training in malaria case management for all age groups and vulnerable populations, and supervision of health workers and CHWs.
PMI will work with partners to ensure that data being gathered are analyzed and used for making decisions and to better assess needs for supplies, case detection, and treatment at the community level. Implementation of all case management activities, including scale up of pre-referral treatment with rectal artesunate, will be done in coordination and collaboration with the Global Fund. The NMCP coordinates implementing partners (for PMI and Global Fund) to ensure harmonized training for case management and CHWs throughout the country. Historically, PMI

started the training activities in the country, and now Catholic Relief Services (Global Fund's principal recipient) is using the same national pool of trainers and training material in the rest of the country. There is a general agreement between PMI and Global Fund to ensure that commodities and other technical resources are shared if and wherever gaps may be identified. Recently, this was enacted when it became clear that both donors would need to procure the same RDT; the one on which case management training was based. In the past, coordinating donor efforts and implementing partner activities has been a challenge for the national program, but as PMI has scaled up its presence, the NMCP has become better organized, and communication between PMI and Global Fund has become more regular, this issue has improved.

Proposed activities with FY 2016 funding: ($4,600,500)

1. *Rapid diagnostics tests (RDTs):* Procure 4,155,000 RDTs to continue scaling up RDT use in health facilities and in communities via CHWs *($2,160,500)*;
2. *Microscope consumables:* Procure reagents, slides, and spare pieces for existing microscopes in hospitals and health centers *($20,000)*;
3. *AS-AQ*: PMI will procure and distribute approximately 1,400,000 ASAQ treatments *($675,000)*;
4. *A/L*: PMI will procure and distribute approximately 600,000 AL treatments *($570,000)*;
5. *Improve malaria diagnostics:* Work with the NMCP and National Laboratory to develop and support a comprehensive quality assurance and quality control plan for malaria diagnostics at all levels of the health system. This will include refresher training for lab technicians (and training on malaria microscopy for new laboratory technicians) and regular supervision of microscopy and RDT performance in health facilities, including systematic review of a predetermined number of positive and negative blood smears, and supervision of RDT performance by CHWs *($100,000)*;
6. *Training/refresher training in RDT use and case management:* Provide refresher training on malaria case management, including diagnosis with correct RDT use at all levels of the health care system of 1,536 healthcare workers and CHWs on malaria case management and 661 healthcare workers on IPTp spread out over 19 hospitals, 152 health centers, and 451 health posts. The current estimate of approximately 2,200 health workers will also include pharmacists and some central-level staff *($325,000)*; and
7. *Supervise health workers and CHWs in RDT use and case management*: Provide integrated, regular supervision of health workers and CHWs focusing on malaria case management, including microscopy and RDT performance. Supervisions will include regular participation from the national, regional (DRS), and provincial (DPS/DCS) level. As part of this activity, PMI will work with the MOH and other key stakeholders such as the Global Fund, to ensure that resources are used to support integrated supervision, and not just malaria *($250,000)*.
8. *BCC for case management*: Funds will be used to support integrated behavior change communication and education activities for communities to improve behaviors related to malaria prevention and treatment. The BCC supported will target prevention activities, including use of ITNs and IPTp. BCC activities will also support appropriate care seeking behavior particularly at the community level through use of CHWs. Emphasis will be

placed on prompt care-seeking for fever and other symptoms of malaria *(Costs covered under BCC section)*;

9. *Community case management*: PMI will provide transport subsidies, reporting tools and other necessary equipment for CHWs, and will support national five NGOs for CHW supervision in Kindia, Boke, and Labe prefectures *($500,000)*.

b. Pharmaceutical management

NMCP/PMI objectives

The objective set forth in the national strategic plan for the pharmaceutical system is to provide treatment to 100% of patients. This overall objective implies supplying quality drugs to health facilities nationwide in sufficient quantities and on a regular basis.

As the main institution in charge of implementing the GOG policy in the pharmaceutical sector, the central medical store *(Pharmacie Central de Guinée-PCG)* was created in 1992 to supply the health facilities nationwide with quality drugs in appropriate quantities and in a timely manner. PCG operates under the administrative oversight of the National Directorate of Pharmacies and Laboratories (DNPL). PCG has established pharmaceutical depots in five of the eight regions in Guinea. This institution has also played a role as sub-recipient of Global Fund grants to procure drugs for the three priority diseases (HIV, tuberculosis, and malaria).

According to the National Pharmaceutical Policy Document, there is one Chinese-owned drug manufacturer in Guinea. Seventy drug wholesalers have been identified as well as 408 private pharmacies, 348 of which are located in the city of Conakry. There are also 38 drug promotion agencies registered by the MOH and 38 drugs sale points registered by the MOH but handled by non-pharmacists. Those pharmacies sell a wide range of antimalarial drugs, including both branded and generic drugs. Drug quality in private pharmacies remains a challenge in Guinea.

Progress since the launch of PMI

Since its launch in FY 2011, PMI has clearly identified the PCG as the main institution to strengthen in order to ensure a smooth distribution of drugs to end users. To assist the pharmaceutical system (mainly PCG and the DNPL) meeting the challenges of timely distribution of quality drugs to the health facilities, PMI efforts have the objective of reinforcing each of the critical functions of these entities (storage, distribution, logistic management information system, and development and enforcement of policies and regulations).

According to the national pharmaceutical policy, the national essential drugs list should be revised every two years. With PMI's support, the DNPL has revised the list twice during the past four years; systematizing the revision process and allowing the DNPL to take responsibility for this activity on a regular basis.

During the past three years, PMI has insistently encouraged PCG officials to implement recommendations from the 2012 assessment conducted by PMI and in 2013 by the European

Union. The onset of the Ebola epidemic has accelerated the need for these reforms and repositioned PCG as the gateway for commodity entry and distribution in the country, and as the unique partner for all donors engaged in supporting the health system.

Progress during the last 12-18 months

In the context of the Ebola epidemic, PMI and the USAID Mission have resolved to focus on providing appropriate support to the PCG to perform its responsibilities, while improving governance of the supply chain and the pharmaceutical system. As a result of the action plan implemented in FY 2014, PMI worked with its key partners including the DNPL, NMCP, and PCG to provide appropriate support to face the challenges of the pharmaceutical system.

Support to the DNPL:

With the DNPL, PMI supported the development and validation of a new National Pharmaceutical Policy with a five-year master plan for its implementation. PMI provided training on legislation, regulations on WHO's good pharmaceutical practices as well as support to revise the national legislation, regulations and organogram. With PMI's support, the DNPL also reorganized its registration division to conform to international norms and developed a logistics management information system (LMIS) for antimalarials, integrated management of childhood illness and family planning commodities as well as other cost recovery commodities. Support was also provided to pharmacists at the regional and prefecture levels to improve pharmaceutical management and LMIS.

Support to the NMCP:

PMI supported the development of epidemiological and consumption data (collection, processing and verification), the issuance of quarterly bulletins on malaria in the regions, end-use verification surveys, and training sessions for the commodities technical working group to perform quantification, consumption management, and development of annual work plans. Also, PMI supported the monitoring and evaluation technical working group to improve integrated supervision and data verification. Overall, PMI contributed to strengthening coordination capacity of the NMCP with other partners, which resulted in the development of an integrated work plan.

Support to PCG:

Given the challenges identified in past years, which prompted the development of a work plan agreed upon by PCG officials, PMI provided extensive support including training on and development of good pharmaceuticals distribution practices, revision of a standard procedures manual, and the creation of a quality assurance unit with self-inspection using WHO norms. As a result of PMI assistance to PCG, commodities storage conditions have considerably improved as testified by the Managing Director and witnessed by the MOP Team during its visit in March 2015. To assist PCG with a clear vision to meet future challenges, PMI supported the development of five-year strategic plan which reflects lessons learned from malaria control in the context of the Ebola epidemic. On the GOG's request, PMI participated in the development of the health sector revival plan, a reference document designed to reinforce service provision and help the health system recover from the Ebola epidemic. To help PCG improve governance and promote transparency and accountability in its operations, PMI supported the elaboration of procurement procedures allowing open competition in tenders. As a result, a competitive process was applied for commodities procurement on behalf of the GOG for the first time in many years. A governance improvement system set up with PMI's support includes provision and use of strategic decision making tool regarding financial management.

Plan and justification

With FY 2016 funding, PMI will continue its catalyst role in assisting with creating conditions to improve the management of the pharmaceutical system. Given the challenges that remain with both the DNPL and PCG, PMI will increase its support to the supply chain and the pharmaceutical sector. PMI support will mainly focus on improving the logistic management information system.

Efforts will also continue, in collaboration with PCG and the DNPL, to strengthen the pharmaceutical sector through supporting reforms to enable the supply chain to perform its core duties of storing and distributing commodities on a regular basis to health facilities and in accordance with international norms and standards. The essential drugs list will be updated with PMI support and will be closely monitored by the DNPL. PMI will also strengthen the drugs regulatory capacity of the DNPL to improve the control over the pharmaceutical sector by well-trained staff. Finally, support to pharmaceutical supplies management will be the centerpiece of PMI support in the coming year to significantly reduce recurrent drug stock outs at health facility and community levels.

The PMI partner will sign an agreement with PCG to ensure that roles and responsibilities with regard to the implementation of the work plan are clearly delineated and understood by all parties involved. PMI will also continue its support to supervision at the regional medical stores as well as supervision of malaria commodity management in health facilities.

In support of NMCP efforts to assure effective donor coordination, PMI and Global Fund – as the main malaria commodity donors in country – distribute commodities in their respective focus areas of the country. This increases efficiency and ensures the whole country is covered. In practice this means that if a depot located in a designated PMI zone is requesting resupply of ACTs, then the PMI implementing partner would ensure the delivery of these ACTs to the depot. The ACTs would be delivered regardless of which donor paid for them; so, the PMI implementing partner could deliver Global Fund-procured ACTs and vice versa. Neither the PMI partner nor Global Fund partner distribute exclusively the commodities that they purchase; as noted, all commodities are compiled and distribution plans are based on which donor implementing partner's designated zone has the need.

The PMI implementing partner will distribute malaria commodities via the PCG from the central level all the way to health facilities. The budget is based on the estimate proposed by the NMCP and the PCG, whereby PMI agreed to pay 5% of the commodity cost to cover storage, handling, and distribution. Since 2015 is the first year for implementation of this agreement, PMI will closely monitor the management and distribution costs in conjunction with our implementing partner. If necessary, PMI will consider reprogramming funds next year in order to continue to ensure distribution of malaria commodities nationwide.

Proposed activities with FY 2016 funding: ($1,150,000)

1. *Improving logistic management information systems*: Continue support to strengthen the logistic management information systems enabling the pharmaceutical system to collect, compile, and process consumption data throughout the health system to improve the forecasting, the procurement, and the distribution of commodities. This activity includes procurement of computers, support for internet connectivity, and capacity building for quantification at the central level (PCG, DNPL), as well as at the regional, prefecture, and district levels *($250,000)*;
2. *Pharmaceutical systems reform*: Continue to support the reform of regulations governing the supply chain management and the pharmaceutical system, including the implementation of the recommendations of the audit performed by the European Union (EU). Reforms are required not only at the central level but also to the periphery in how stocks are managed. PMI's support of the EU audit findings and recommendations will be linked to this activity *($200,000)*;
3. *Improve drug regulatory capacity*: Continue to support improvement of the regulatory and oversight capacities of the DNPL, revision of national list of essential drugs, and enhanced control of compliance to the pharmaceutical policy and regulations by PCG and the private pharmacies network. Capacity building of the pharmaceutical system will include improving capacity to combat counterfeit drugs and the illicit sale of drugs. *($100,000)*;
4. *Management of pharmaceutical supplies*: Manage the distribution of PMI commodities down to the health facility level, including warehousing, transportation, storage and distribution. Cost estimate is based on 5% of the commodity cost (per NMCP and PCG) *($300,000)*; and,
5. *Strengthen pharmaceutical storage capacity*: This activity will build upon current PMI support to PCG in order to provide additional equipment and material, improving commodities storage conditions at the central level as well as at regional level *($300,000)*.

5. Health systems strengthening and capacity building

PMI/NMCP objectives

The national strategic plan aims at controlling malaria to promote a sustainable social and economic development of the country. Hence, the MOH has assigned the NMCP the mission of providing the Guinean population with universal access to quality malaria care in accordance with the national health policy. The national health policy also recommends that universal access to malaria care for the people of Guinea should be supported by values such as social justice, solidarity, equity, ethics, probity, and quality.

Moreover, the new malaria strategic plan endorses good governance principles, gender equality, consideration for evidence-based practices, and recommendations provided by international institutions in charge of malaria control, mainly the WHO. Those principles are reflected in various documents adopted by regional organizations including the African Union and the Economic Community of West African States and adhered to by the GOG, and include:

- Promote the national malaria control policy based on the Roll Back Malaria (RBM) partnership principles;
- Reinforce the epidemiological surveillance system for malaria control through data collection and analysis for decision making;
- Strengthen behavior change communication among the population in order to promote extensive use of malaria prevention measures and treatment products;
- Elaborate, monitor, and evaluate implementation of the national malaria strategic plan on an annual basis;
- Mobilize and manage human, financial and material resources necessary for the implementation of the national malaria strategic plan; and
- Promote and develop partnerships with all stakeholders in the control of malaria.

The achievement of the goal set forth by the malaria strategic plan calls for the following specific objectives:

- Ensure protection of at least 80% of the population with effective malaria prevention measures;
- Ensure biological confirmation of 90% of malaria cases;
- Provide an early and correct treatment of 90% of malaria cases;
- Reinforce the monitoring and evaluation system at all levels, in accordance with the revised monitoring and evaluation plan; and
- Strengthen the management (planning and coordination) capabilities of the NMCP.

Progress since the launch of PMI

The Guinean health system, already weakened by insufficient number of qualified human resources in health facilities, has been confronted with further damages since the Ebola epidemic started in December 2013. In addition to the shortage of staff, the Ebola epidemic decreased the capacity of the health system to offer malaria services due to absenteeism of health workers and fear of Ebola contamination at health facilities as well as at the community level. A rapid survey conducted in December 2014 to assess the impact of Ebola on malaria service provision revealed that use of malaria services has significantly decreased in Ebola-affected zones. MOH officials, with support from partners including PMI, developed a health system revival plan designed not only to strengthen the health system and allow it to meet the needs of the population, but most importantly, to convince the population to return to health facilities to seek care. The GOG plans on mobilizing internal and external resources for rolling out the health system revival plan, the cornerstones of which will be CHWs and rebuilding trust among care users.

Despite the contextual challenges of the Ebola epidemic, PMI continued its support of the NMCP to build coordination and leadership capacity. Following the organizational assessment conducted in 2013, PMI shared the findings with all malaria stakeholders including the Global Fund principal recipient. In addition to providing support to address operational and technical weaknesses, PMI has posted a Malaria Advisor to the NMCP through the Leadership and Management Grant mechanism. The contribution of this expertise to the improvement of NMCP day-to-day and prospective operations, such as activities planning and development of appropriate documents required by the Global Fund, have been unanimously appreciated by the NMCP's leadership.

The findings of the assessment conducted by PMI have prompted the Global Fund to participate in the capacity building efforts, allowing the NMCP to work toward the day when it could again become a principal recipient of the Global Fund. As a result, the Global Fund has decided to fund some key positions within the NMCP including those related to financial management, accounting, supply chain management, and monitoring and evaluation.

Progress during the last 12-18 Months

During the past 12-18 months, PMI supported malaria donors' coordination through the RBM partnership framework. Meetings were held on a quarterly basis and support for dissemination of meeting outcomes to malaria stakeholders was provided. Dialogue with the NMCP, the Global Fund and other partners continued to build the management capacity of the NMCP in order to allow it achieve its objectives in the context of the Ebola epidemic.

As indicated in the pharmaceutical management section, PMI has provided catalytic support during the past twelve months to the supply chain and pharmaceutical system to play the roles they are assigned by the GOG. Most importantly, the PCG's operations have considerably improved due to PMI's support and the DNPL has also engaged in strengthening its regulatory framework to conform to international norms.

Support to technical working groups continued, mainly diagnosis, behavior change communication, and monitoring and evaluation. PMI supported organization of RBM quarterly meetings and enabled continuous exchanges among malaria control partners as these meetings were deemed indispensable in the context of the Ebola epidemic.

PMI continued building the entomological capacity of the NMCP. Support was provided to start the renovation of the insectarium, conduct entomological surveillance as well as sponsor two NMCP staff members entomological training at the Center of Entomological Research of Cotonou in Benin.

Efforts to assist the NMCP to build a reliable malaria database linked to the national health management information system continue with support from various partners including the Global Fund and PMI. With support from PMI, the revised monitoring and evaluation plan — an integral part of the new malaria strategic plan — will improve malaria program performance metrics and enable timely decision-making. PMI has also conducted a needs assessment to strengthen the capacity of the National Laboratory for drug quality control. An action plan is being developed to build the country capacity to test quality of imported drugs.

To support the NMCP's day-to-day operations, PMI continued to provide internet connection as well as office equipment such as computers and USB keys.

Plan and justification

Given the challenges posed to the health system by the Ebola epidemic and the political commitment shown by the GOG in rebuilding the health system, PMI will continue supporting key activities designed to contribute to strengthening the health system and create conditions for increased access and use of malaria services. PMI will continue emphasizing capacity building at the NMCP, in coordination with its partners and other donors such as the Global Fund. In the aftermath of the Ebola epidemic, actions will include advocacy and involvement of MOH high level officials to implement the health system revival plan that will have a direct impact on increasing access and use of malaria services offered in health facilities as well as in communities. The health recovery plan (2015-2017) which is part of the national health development plan (2015-2024) was developed in consultation with all the stakeholders and integrates the resources of other priority prevention and disease control programs such as HIV, MCH, reproductive health, family planning, etc., and focuses on three main priority areas: 1) elimination and control of Ebola, 2) strengthening of the health district system, 3) and improved governance in the health sector.

With FY 2016 funding, PMI will continue supporting the NMCP to conduct supervision and provide logistics support including office materials, communication capacity through internet connectivity, and M&E system strengthening.

PMI will also continue its partnership with Peace Corps Guinea to work on malaria at the community level. Peace Corps Response Volunteers are usually third-year volunteers or volunteers who have previously completed their service and have applied for a Response Volunteer position, generally with an NGO or to coordinate and lead other volunteers' activities related to a specific health project. Peace Corps' *Stomp out Malaria* program is active in Guinea and PMI has benefited from volunteers' activities at the community level with coordination and assistance from the Response Volunteer. Given the current pipeline and due to the fact that Peace Corps Volunteers have been evacuated in 2014 to the United States during the Ebola epidemic, PMI did not program any new funding to Peace Corps during the FY 2016 MOP planning, although the MOP planning team paid a visit to Peace Corps' office in Conakry and discussed pending activities and future plans.

Proposed activities with FY 2016 funding: ($200,000)

1. *Management support for NMCP*: Support to the NMCP to assist them in team building, logistics and supervision, office management including communication capacity/connectivity, and M&E systems strengthening *($150,000)*; and
2. *Training and capacity building of NMCP*: Support to NMCP to build capacity via conference and workshop attendance, both national and international, and to improve program management in M&E as well as BCC *($50,000)*.

6. Behavior change communication

NMCP/PMI objectives

In the updated national strategic plan, the NMCP highlights the important role of behavior change communication (BCC) across interventions by specifying an objective related to adoption of target behaviors for malaria control and prevention. The first target for the objective is to develop and disseminate a coordinated communication plan for all relevant partners in Guinea. The strategy also highlights the important role of a partnership to coordinate BCC messages, tools, and processes, including pre-testing, validation, and distribution of support materials.

The NMCP developed a communication plan in 2009, which was revised with PMI support in March 2012 (to cover the period 2012-2015). The plan emphasizes comprehensive communication activities based on formative research, including interpersonal and mass media approaches, supported through training and educational materials and appropriately monitored and evaluated. It also identifies key behaviors and describes challenges, barriers, and opportunities for adoption of those behaviors. The plan will be updated again using data from the recent Knowledge, Attitudes, and Practices (KAP) survey (September 2014). Updates will focus on revising messaging and communication approaches to better address barriers and gaps identified in various audience segments (e.g., heads of household, pregnant women, mothers).

A technical committee for BCC has convened, but its initial efforts have been side-tracked by the ongoing Ebola epidemic. In the long run, this group will be central to ensuring consistent messaging, harmonizing training approaches, and implementing activities in a complementary way. In addition to PMI, the Global Fund provides support for BCC activities related to malaria prevention and case management. While donor efforts are coordinated at the national level, PMI and Global Fund each have geographical areas (zones) which they support as part of the geographical distribution of roles and responsibilities between PMI and Global Fund. PMI supports BCC activities in PMI zones and Global Fund supports activities in the remainder of the country. The NMCP is currently developing a communication plan that will include BCC activities in all areas.

Progress since PMI was launched

PMI progress on BCC to date has included revising the NMCP's national communication plan and training manual used by animators for BCC techniques related to malaria prevention and treatment. The national communication plan, training materials, and tools are used not only in PMI target areas, but also by the Global Fund implementers in the remaining areas of the country. PMI has also supported training of NGO animators on BCC related to malaria prevention, and supported Peace Corps volunteers to work with local NGOs on implementing malaria BCC activities in the region of Boke and Conakry.

Early PMI-supported activities for BCC primarily focused on increasing ANC attendance and IPTp uptake, as well as increasing early care seeking for fever. These PMI activities were part of an integrated mechanism for family and child health in PMI zones, and included both interpersonal communication through peer discussion groups, as well as mass media through radio, television, and pamphlet distribution. With the new PMI bilateral program, BCC focused almost exclusively on the ITN universal coverage campaign to ensure ITN hang-up and continuing use post-campaign before once again expanding its scope to also focus on case management and malaria in pregnancy.

Case management training for health workers and CHWs included a BCC component and CHWs were given job aid posters and storyboards to conduct sensitization sessions on malaria prevention and treatment in their communities. In order to improve the population's knowledge on malaria treatment, PMI in collaboration with the NMCP produced and disseminated 20,000 pamphlets in the 151 health centers covered by PMI and produced and disseminated one malaria prevention TV spot in French and local languages. PMI trained members of health and hygiene committees and facilitators to conduct group discussions and mass awareness talks on the prevention and treatment of malaria. This activity resulted in 1,884 group discussions and mass sensitizations during which over 75,000 people were reached, including almost 43,000 women. During these discussions, CHW and non-governmental organizations (NGO) facilitators emphasized key messages to the population including the importance of seeking health care in case of fever, and the availability of free malaria testing and treatment.

Since the Ebola epidemic began, PMI has had to revise its BCC approach to address malaria in the context of the epidemic. This has included training a larger number of people including community members about the importance of using ITNs and seeking treatment for fever, in addition to the standard package of BCC activities like radio spots, posters and CHW mobilization. Addressing malaria in the context of Ebola is essential not only to continue preventing and treating malaria cases, but to also reduce the number of febrile cases, and thus suspected Ebola cases in the community. Reducing the number of suspected Ebola cases helps reduce the strain on an already overburdened health system, in addition to reducing the risk that those non-Ebola febrile cases awaiting triage in Ebola transit centers will contract Ebola.

Progress during the last 12-18 months

BCC activities focused heavily on the completion of ITN distribution in the area of Conakry. This was the last remaining location to be reached as part of the universal coverage campaign that began in May 2013, but was not completed due to a variety of reasons including delay in arrival of PMI ITNs, local elections in November 2013, and the onset of the Ebola epidemic. As a follow-up to the universal coverage campaign, BCC activities are aimed at proper care and use of nets, and household hang-up visits in PMI target zones. The campaign slogan, *"The entire family, every night, all year, let's sleep under mosquito nets!"* was the foundation of the Conakry distribution and national post-campaign communication strategy, which included a mix of mass media: SMS, TV, and radio including round table discussions; mid-media: theater troupes, concerts, and banners at special events; and interpersonal communications: household visits for enumeration and post-distribution hang-up. A total of 13,889 people were trained on social mobilization for the Conakry distribution and national post-campaign efforts.

In addition to nets, PMI validated and distributed a report on the Knowledge Attitude and Practice (KAP) survey, developed a malaria bulletin in collaboration with the NMCP, and trained 17 journalists in Kindia region on key malaria messages.

The results of a KAP survey (conducted August-September 2014 with PMI support), which included a qualitative component, will be used to better understand target audiences' attitudes and behaviors around malaria and to update the national malaria communication plan. Survey outcome indicators aligned with the RBM-recommended BCC malaria indicators are summarized along with DHS 2012 data in the table below. More detailed results are summarized in this paragraph. In terms of exposure to awareness messages, the survey showed that about 60% of household heads have heard or seen a message about malaria in the last six months preceding the survey. This proportion is almost the same in urban and rural areas. Messages that affected much of the population are those related to the danger of malaria, its mode of transmission, the protection methods, and the importance of sleeping under a mosquito net. The survey also showed that about 57% of women aged 15 to 49 that are pregnant or have a child less than 5 years old (i.e., eligible women) appear to have been affected by malaria messages during the last six months preceding the survey. In terms of knowledge of signs of severe malaria, the main signs of severe malaria cited by heads of households are high fever (55.6%), vomiting (45%), and fever (44.9%). In terms of knowledge of prevention methods, the use of the net as a malaria prevention method was a widely known means (83.1%), followed by cleanliness (51%). Those who cited preventive treatment, repellents, and insecticides were respectively 21.4%, 18.6% and 15.7%. Among eligible women, the most known prevention methods are nets (81.8%), cleanliness (58.9%), and preventive treatment (17.9%). However, a significant proportion of household heads (19.5%) cited the wrong modality, not eating bad foods as a means of prevention. This proportion was 18.4% among eligible women. In addition, the survey results are being translated into revised BCC tools and materials, which will be used to provide updated refresher training for CHWs and health facility teams, improved mass media packages, targeted interpersonal communication and community outreach using CHWs and local NGOs, and supervision and monitoring of BCC efforts aimed at increasing health facility utilization.

Table IX: Evolution of Key BCC Malaria Indicators in Guinea from 2012 to 2014

Outcome Indicators	Baseline[16]	Follow-up
Proportion of respondents who slept under an ITN the previous night	DHS 2012 (18.9%)	KAP 2014[17] (65.0%)
Proportion of respondents who received two or more doses of IPTp during an ANC visit during pregnancy completed within the last two years	DHS 2012 (17.8%)	KAP 2014 (92.4%)
Proportion of respondents who sought advice or treatment for fever in children under five years of age	DHS 2012 (37.1%)	KAP 2014 (83.9%)
Proportion of respondents who recall hearing or seeing any malaria message within the last six months	DHS 2012 (Not reported)	KAP 2014 (57.7%)
Proportion of respondents who know the cause of, symptoms of, treatment for, or preventive measures for malaria	DHS 2012 (*)	KAP 2014 (*)
Proportion of respondents who feel confident in their ability to perform a specific malaria-related behavior	KAP 2014 (66.3%)	TBD

Cause (mosquito bite): 85.0% vs. 89.1%
Symptom (fever): 66.6% vs. 69.3%
Treatment (ACT): Not reported
Prevention -   Mosquito net: 36.5% vs. 89.1%
* ITN: 41.2% vs. Not reported*
* Preventive medication: 25.9% vs. 21.4%*

In general, the country is still focused on getting to zero Ebola cases and consequently, has not spent a significant amount of time on post-Ebola planning. However, there have been discussions among partners, including the NMCP, that the approach to address the impact of Ebola on malaria should be two-fold: community and health facility levels. PMI partners have intensified their support to CHWs by incorporating information on Ebola, implementing new case management guidelines, providing gloves, and supporting social mobilization. In the future, PMI will continue close supervision of CHWs, and will also strengthen our collaboration with Health and Hygiene Committees. At the health facility level, PMI partners will be training HCWs in case management and infection prevention and control, and providing basic universal protection commodities such as gloves. The PMI team will work to leverage existing Ebola funds for malaria, including potential Ebola Supplemental Funding.

Plan and justification

PMI will continue to support the NMCP's communication plan with implementation of BCC activities in PMI target zones reflecting NMCP priorities and national policies, including ITN use, ANC attendance and IPTp uptake, and case management, including RDT and ACT use, as well as malaria in the context of Ebola. Proposed activities will continue to reflect a mix of interpersonal communication approaches and mass media.

---

[16]DHS 2012 data are available by region but not shown here; these data represent national estimates.

[17] The KAP survey was conducted August-September 2014 in the PMI target area to collect outcome data at the prefecture level. Though the baseline is not directly comparable, it will provide an idea of the potential impact of the intervention.

Discussions about a new date for the MIS that was scheduled for 2014 but postponed due to Ebola are ongoing. The MIS will collect information on key behavior and knowledge indicators, including many that were measured during the 2014 KAP survey. The survey may also be able to provide greater clarity on the perceptions, knowledge levels, behaviors, social and economic barriers, and behavior determinants of target populations, especially pregnant women and young children, to understand factors underlying uptake and use of ITNs and malaria services. Based on the results of these data collection activities, some BCC activities may be targeted to children as message agents with integration of malaria communication tools into schools.

Efforts to increase CHW and health facility staff effectiveness through interpersonal communication tools may also be intensified, especially in the current context of the Ebola epidemic, which has led to a loss of confidence in the public health sector by the population, and in reduced or non-performance of health facility workers due to fear. Also, CHWs in Ebola-affected areas have been unintentionally diverted from their regular duties (including community case management of malaria), as they are being paid to trace Ebola-case contacts. Thus, greater communication and supervision efforts need to be employed to overcome these obstacles to improving malaria prevention and treatment practices.

Proposed activities with FY 2016 funding: ($300,000)

1. *BCC for ITNs, IPTp, and case management:* BCC will be part of a communication package including ITN use, IPTp uptake, and case management at the health facility and community levels. Activities will be focused in PMI target zones but will be consistent with the NMCP's national communication plan and national policies, and coordinated with BCC activities in the rest of the country, in particular, those that relate to malaria in the context of Ebola and will be part of the USAID Guinea global BCC strategy *($300,000)*.

7. Monitoring and evaluation

NMCP/PMI objectives

Monitoring and evaluation is a key component of Guinea's malaria program, and the NMCP recognizes the importance of having a strong monitoring and evaluation (M&E) strategy to inform programmatic interventions and measure outcomes and impact. The NMCP finalized its national M&E plan along with the national strategy in February 2014; both documents cover the period 2013-2017.

The new plan identifies indicators, targets, and data sources and emphasizes data collection, data quality assurance, and dissemination and use of data.[18] Specific M&E priorities reflected in the updated plan include revising and maintaining the national malaria database, including the health management and information system (HMIS) and supervision data; creating and disseminating malaria bulletins; building M&E capacity at regional and district levels; and strengthening

---

[18]A full indicator table is available in Annex 6 of the National Strategic Plan.

relationships with partners collecting malaria data, including HMIS and the Integrated Disease Surveillance and Response system. A technical committee for M&E at the national level is led by the NMCP and made up of donor and partner representatives including PMI, and its partners, Catholic Relief Services (for Global Fund), and WHO, among others; the consistency of meetings has been impacted by the Ebola crisis.

Currently, the following data sources collect malaria data in Guinea:

- *Monthly malaria reporting tool:* Starting in late 2013 the NMCP, with the support of the MOH unit responsible for HMIS, implemented a new monthly reporting tool to collect malaria commodity and epidemiological data on the same form. First rolled out in PMI zones, the monthly reporting tool was expanded to the Global Fund zones starting in mid-2014. Since the annual HMIS report is not perceived as a timely or valid data source (the most recent report is from 2011), and indeed the HMIS has essentially become nonfunctional during the Ebola crisis, the new monthly malaria report is the primary source of data for the NMCP. It currently is providing key malaria data with 80% reporting completeness in the zones that have been targeted for training and supervision by PMI, with lower completeness in the Global Fund zones. The reporting tools are filled out at health centers and report data on malaria case management, including the number of total consultations and the number of suspect cases and confirmed cases seen at health centers and their affiliated health posts and community health workers, as well as data on stock and monthly consumption of malaria commodities. The monthly reports are then digitized at the health district level and sent electronically to the NMCP.
- *Integrated Disease Surveillance and Response system:* Supported by WHO, Guinea's weekly Integrated Disease Surveillance and Response system is based at the Division of Prevention and Disease Control at the MOH. It consists of weekly, telephone-based reporting on ten diseases, including malaria. While a timely tool for routine malaria data, it lacks key indicators, does not stratify by age, does not include data on completeness, and does not generally include data from health posts and community health workers.
- *Household surveys:* Guinea has implemented a DHS in 2005 and 2012, a Multiple Indicator Cluster Survey (MICS) in 2007, and Global Fund-supported national coverage surveys conducted in 2009 and 2010 to measure population coverage with basic interventions (ITNs, IPTp, and ACTs), as well as a health facility component assessing commodity availability and case management practices.[19] The 2012 DHS provides follow-up estimates for key malaria indicators, as well as the first national estimates of malaria parasitemia. An MIS planned for 2014 was indefinitely postponed as a result of Ebola and the next DHS will be implemented in 2017. The Global Fund is planning a national household survey to measure intervention coverage in 2015, an activity postponed from 2014 due to the Ebola epidemic. A KAP survey was implemented in August and September 2014 to provide formative data on malaria-related behaviors including net use and treatment-seeking practices.
- *Health facility surveys:* Three kinds of surveys provide data on malaria case management in health facilities. All three data collection activities are being closely coordinated to

---

[19] The 2005 DHS data are available, but the 2007 MICS results are not maintained by UNICEF headquarters; they may be available in country. The reports from the 2009 and 2010 Global Fund surveys are available.

ensure complementary data capture and avoid duplication of efforts: 1) PMI-funded, semiannual (originally quarterly) End-use verification (EUV) surveys have been implemented starting in 2012, with five to date. These surveys provide data on malaria commodity availability and malaria case management based on a convenience sample of health facilities on a regular basis; 2) Yearly health facility surveys with random sampling of health facilities provide detailed, representative, national-level data on healthcare worker performance regarding malaria case management, and guide national healthcare worker training strategies. The first such survey was implemented in December 2014; 3) The Service Availability and Readiness Assessment (SARA) survey is a large, standardized health facility survey that covers a broad range of healthcare delivery services. In Guinea, a SARA survey has been planned with support from the Global Fund, the Global Alliance for Vaccines and Immunizations, WHO, and PMI. Though not a malaria-specific survey, the SARA includes indicators on health facility readiness to provide malaria services, including health worker training, supervision, and malaria commodity availability. Moreover, the survey committee is considering piloting a "Malaria Module," consisting of a patient exit interview, in a subset of the sampled facilities. Originally planned for 2014, the SARA survey has been delayed to 2015 or later due to the Ebola epidemic.

The table below summarizes existing malaria data sources in Guinea as well as anticipated data collection activities through 2017.

Table X: Health Systems Strengthening Activities

Data Source	M&E Activities	Year								
		'09	'10	'11	'12	'13	'14	'15	'16	'17
Household surveys	Demographic Health Survey (DHS)				X					X
	Malaria Indicator Survey (MIS)							X?		
	Global Fund national coverage survey	X*	X*					X*		
	KAP survey						X			
Health Facility Surveys	SARA survey							X		
	Health facility survey						X		X	X
	EUV survey					3X	2X	2X	2X	2X
Malaria surveillance and routine system support	Routine system support					X	X	X	X	X
Therapeutic	Therapeutic efficacy study				X*			X	X	X
Entomology	Entomological surveillance and resistance monitoring					X	X	X	X	X
Other Data Sources	ITN durability monitoring							X	X	X

*Not PMI funded

Progress since PMI was launched

Routine data and HMIS strengthening: The *Bureau de Stratégie et de Développement (BSD)* and the NMCP have collaborated, with the support of PMI, to revise monthly malaria reporting to capture key epidemiological and stock management data on one form. The revised form includes the following indicators: number of suspect malaria cases, cases tested (stratified by microscopy and RDT), cases confirmed positive (stratified by microscopy and RDT), cases treated with ACT, severe cases treated, cases referred, and deaths among severe cases. Numbers are reported for the health facility, as well as by CHWs. Data are also included from ANC including total women seen in ANC, number receiving first dose of SP, number receiving at least three doses of

SP, and number of women sensitized at ANC. The revised forms have been introduced throughout the country as of mid-2014.

The monthly malaria report was derived from the existing HMIS tool by adding commodities (drugs, RDTs, and nets) data and revising the epidemiological data elements. A copy of the malaria monthly report is sent to the NMCP and national HMIS office. The NMCP has developed its own data management system and efforts are underway to revitalize the HMIS system that is expected to be housed under the BSD. The BSD Director General and the Health Information and Research Division Chief positions that manage the production of the HMIS have been vacant for the past two years and no national reports have been produced since 2011. There is a coordinated donor effort (e.g., USAID, EU, GAVI, WB, Global Fund and UNICEF) working with the MOH to strengthen the BSD. In addition to personnel issues there is a focus on integrating and/or coordinating existing program information systems (e.g., malaria, HIV/AIDS, EPI, TB and the Ebola Coordination), transitioning to the open source DHIS2 platform adopted by the Global Fund, USAID, PEPFAR and Economic Community Of West African States (ECOWAS) member states as the regional HMIS database, providing adequate GOG budget support, and the production and use of quality information for management and planning. In terms of HMIS coordination with related health information systems, USAID also plans to use Ebola recovery and other funds to support the development of LMIS and HRIS/mHero platforms within PCG which does not currently have viable operational procedures for personnel management, inventory control beyond the regional level, procurement, accounting, and finances.

Currently, commodity reporting data come from multiple complementary (but not duplicative) reporting systems. The monthly malaria reporting tool provides regular data from health facility registers and the hope is that these data will eventually be integrated into a functional HMIS. The end-use verification survey (see below) provides more in-depth cross-sectional commodity availability data for a convenience sample of health facilities in the country at two points during the year. The PCG complements these two data collection efforts with quarterly commodity inventories to assess commodity ordering and distribution practices in the field (See table below).

EUV Survey: Five EUV surveys have been conducted to date: January 2013, April 2013, September 2013, July 2014, and December 2014. The first survey found relatively high levels of ACT stockouts in the previous three months (50-100% of facilities sampled), but showed better results for ACT stocks on the day of the survey due to a recent PMI emergency procurement and distribution. Additional results showed that only 36% of staff were trained in case management; roughly half of all malaria cases were diagnosed based on clinical symptoms alone; and one-third of these cases did not receive an appropriate antimalarial. The second survey, conducted in April 2013, showed better results for ACT stocks due to additional PMI distributions. However, RDTs were still not widely available in facilities, resulting in clinical diagnosis for cases. The survey conducted in September 2013 showed improvement in stock availability, but suggested that there were still considerable gaps in case management practices. Approximately one-third of cases still received a clinical diagnosis and 23% of cases did not receive the appropriate treatment. The fourth survey, carried out in July 2014, showed continued availability of malaria commodities, but also stressed case management problems, particularly at the health facility level. This survey also noted data quality issues, a concern also highlighted during the fifth EUV survey (see below). While the first three EUV surveys were carried out exclusively in PMI zones, the fourth and fifth EUV surveys were expanded to include health facilities in Global Fund zones.

A table summarizing commodity data sources and data collection methods in Guinea is provided below.

Table XI. Monitoring and Evaluation Data Sources

Data source	Method of collection	Frequency	Method of reporting
Monthly reporting tool	Uses the patient registers and commodity dispensing registers	Monthly	Paper- based at the health center, digitalized and compiled at the health district and electronically sent to the NMCP and the HMIS
End-Use verification	Patient registers, commodity orders and distribution registers, inspection of condition of the commodities and the storage space	Bi-annually	Paper-based at the health facilities, digitalized at the central level
Inventory by the PCG	Uses questionnaires used by a team of pharmacists from the central and regional levels and looks at the commodity ordering and distribution registers	Quarterly	Paper-based at the decentralized level but digitalized and compiled at the central level

2012 DHS: The 2012 DHS was implemented from June-October 2012 and provided the first nationally representative estimates of malaria parasitemia. Because it was implemented in the rainy season, these estimates will be comparable to the MIS, originally planned for 2014 but now postponed due to Ebola. Additionally, the DHS provides important baseline measures for ITN coverage and use because it was implemented prior to the 2013 mass ITN distribution campaign. A Global Fund-financed household coverage survey will provide important coverage and use estimate updates when implemented in 2015/2016.

Therapeutic Efficacy Studies: Researchers at the Maferinyah Research and Training Center conducted a therapeutic efficacy study for Guinea's first-line ACT, AS-AQ, with data collection from 2011-2012 (not PMI-funded). The study generally followed the WHO protocol, used a 28-day follow-up period, and was funded by the European & Developing Countries Clinical Trials Partnership. Unpublished results show 97% efficacy for AS-AQ in children and adults. The

Maferinyah Research and Training Center is also conducting a three-arm clinical trial of artesunate-pyronaridine, artesunate-piperaquine, and AS-AQ. The Maferinyah researchers have also begun a study aimed at examining the seasonal burden of malaria (in low transmission and high transmission seasons) in the four different natural regions of Guinea (coastal, middle, high, and forested). The data collection will include entomological parameters, as well as individuals' knowledge, attitudes, and practices related to malaria prevention and treatment.

Progress during the last 12-18 months

Completion rates for monthly reporting in the areas supported by PMI have remained stable at above 80%. Starting mid-2014, the malaria-specific monthly reporting system has been introduced into the areas supported by the Global Fund, but reporting completeness in these areas has been a challenge, with less than half of health districts regularly submitting their reports. The NMCP has identified data completeness to be the first of two grand challenges for malaria M&E in Guinea.

The second grand challenge for malaria M&E is poor data quality. Health facility supervisory visits have continued to find significant discrepancies between data recorded on monthly reports and data found in health facility registers. As a result, the NMCP has been reluctant to rely solely on the monthly reporting data to guide decision making.

To address these challenges, quarterly regional meetings throughout the country have provided an opportunity for key persons from the health facility, district, regional, and national levels to discuss progress and challenges with the new reporting system, common data quality issues, and ideas for data use at lower levels. Practical sessions focused on presentation of epidemiological and pharmaceutical management data. Awards (laptops, printers, and scanners) were presented to the top-performing districts for reporting. These quarterly meetings will continue to support routine data collection and reporting, encourage data quality improvements, and provide technical assistance for data use.

Further progress on addressing data quality issues was made with the development and introduction of a unified malaria supervision guide. The comprehensive guide covers all areas of malaria activities at the health center, including malaria commodity management, IPTp, laboratory diagnosis, patient examination, malaria treatment, registry completion, and monthly malaria report completion. The goal is that all supervisory visits related to malaria use the malaria supervision guide, thus standardizing malaria supervision and guaranteeing uniformly comprehensive supervision throughout the country. The supervision guide was piloted in late 2014, and regular supervisions using the guide have been ongoing throughout the country since early 2015.

Starting in October 2014, the NMCP has been issuing monthly malaria bulletins. These short, two-page reports summarize the current epidemiological state of malaria in Guinea, presenting 11 key indicators for each health district. They are disseminated to NMCP staff, key partners, and regional and prefectural health offices. Concurrently, monthly commodity reports are generated by the NMCP M&E team and shared internally within the NMCP. These reports provide commodity data at the health center and health district level, including the total amount of available stock, the average monthly consumption, and the months of stock left for each malaria commodity.

The MIS was originally planned for 2014 to include data collection during the peak transmission months of June and July. An in-country steering group, with technical assistance from the partner implementing the survey, had worked to develop the timeline, sampling strategy, and questionnaire. The Ebola epidemic, declared in March 2014, prompted stakeholders and the NMCP to reconsider the survey timeline. With the main concerns around risk to data collectors and community perceptions of the data collection – particularly for the blood draws required for biomarkers – the potential for abnormally high refusal rates and poor data quality, in addition to safety concerns, were too high to justify continuing with the survey in 2014. The MIS steering committee decided to provisionally postpone the survey to high-transmission season in 2015, but with cases remaining in 2015, the MIS is still on hold and will not take place in 2015.

A KAP survey was carried out in August and September 2014 in randomly selected households in PMI zones. Ownership of at least one bed net in households with a pregnant woman or children under five was found to be 84%. Overall, 72% of pregnant women and 70% of children under five were reported to have slept under a bed net the night before the interview. Between 90-95% of interviewed household members identified mosquito bites as the cause of malaria, and the majority of heads of household (83%) identified bed nets as a malaria prevention strategy. While around 90% of interviewed household members identified health facilities as the preferred source of care in the face of suspected malaria, only 30% of women reported going to health facilities on the day of the appearance of fever in children under five (additional KAP results are reported in the BCC section).

The EUV surveys have continued to provide useful data on commodities and case management that are well received by the NMCP. During the most recent survey, conducted in December 2014, 31 health facilities and 5 warehouses were visited. Teams found low rates of stockouts of RDTs and ACTs, but high rates of stockouts of injectable artesunate and quinine tablets. While only 41% of staff had been trained on malaria case management, each surveyed facility had at least one person trained on malaria case management. Health facilities reported decreases in health facility attendance due to the Ebola epidemic (additional case management data reported in the Case Management section).

The past year also marked the development of a strategy for antimalarial resistance monitoring in Guinea, in line with WHO guidelines for endemic countries.[20] Led by the NMCP M&E team, a committee chose four sites, one in each natural region of Guinea, to act as sentinel sites for antimalarial resistance monitoring. Therapeutic efficacy studies will be carried out in two sites per year, resulting in a two-year rotation. The first two therapeutic efficacy studies will start in May 2015, and are expected to run for four months. The study protocol was finalized in late 2014 with technical assistance from PMI, and the studies will be implemented by the Maferinyah Rural Health Research Center.

---

[20] World Health Organization (2009) Methods for surveillance of antimalarial drug efficacy. Geneva: WHO: 9.

A health facility survey designed to measure the impact of the Ebola epidemic on malaria case management in Guinea was performed in December 2014. The survey was led by NMCP with technical assistance from PMI, and funded jointly by PMI and the Global Fund. It found substantial disruptions in malaria care delivery due to the Ebola epidemic, including decreases in health facility attendance and in the number of patients treated with antimalarials, and reduced community malaria case management. The survey results have been disseminated with key groups in Guinea; discussions on how best to address the survey findings are ongoing.

In previous MOPs, PMI had proposed to support sentinel surveillance in select health facilities to get facility-based longitudinal data on malaria burden and case management practices (e.g., testing rates). Implementation progress has been slow due to Ebola and difficulty identifying sites that meet selection criteria. In recent consultation with the NMCP, there is agreement that the monthly malaria reporting is sufficiently filling this need for data and sentinel surveillance is no longer a priority activity. The PMI team and implementing partner will work with the NMCP going forward to determine the best use of these funds to support the ongoing facility-based data collection efforts.

Plan and justification

In its sixth year of implementation, PMI will continue to collaborate with the NMCP, donors, and other stakeholders to support M&E for Guinea's national strategic plan. With the 2012 DHS, key malaria baseline indicators for intervention coverage and impact (including parasitemia) are available. The 2015 (or later) MIS will provide essential interim measures for progress, as will the 2017 DHS, partially supported by PMI. PMI will not fund back to back surveys (i.e., 2016 MIS and 2017 DHS), but will instead confer with the NMCP and other donors to determine priorities and reprogram survey funds as needed. PMI support for the 2017 DHS will be a joint contribution with other health sectors in the USAID Mission, as well as other partners (total DHS cost and partner contributions are not yet known at the time of writing). The proposed PMI contribution to the DHS is identical to what was provided for the 2012 DHS. The SARA survey originally to be implemented in late 2014 has been rescheduled for 2015 and will provide nationally representative data on health facility readiness to provide needed malaria services, and potentially some data on malaria case management practices as well (this will depend on final decisions regarding piloting the Malaria Module). Malaria-specific health facility surveys in 2016 and 2017 will assess progress in case management (e.g., adherence to national testing and treatment guidelines), identify if and where gaps remain, and will be used to track changes in malaria care delivery due to the Ebola epidemic. PMI will continue data collection on commodity availability through the EUV survey to provide rapidly available and actionable information for decision makers.

PMI will continue to support routine system strengthening. USAID funded a national assessment of the HMIS (in February 2014), and results were shared at a stakeholders meeting in June 2014 and the report will be the foundation for the development of a strategic plan for routine system strengthening. PMI will contribute to the cross-cutting United States government efforts to strengthen the HMIS and advocate for malaria needs within this broader stakeholder effort. We will use the action-planning process (which will be MOH-led) to identify the key areas where

PMI can have impact for its investment. But we do acknowledge that coordination across MOH disease programs, donors, and implementing partners is a challenge that will take time, especially as priorities have shifted during the current crisis. Until the action-planning process is in place and a clear strategy begins to emerge, PMI will use existing routine system strengthening funds to meet immediate needs that have been identified by the malaria program. Key areas of focus, reflected in the two M&E main challenges as declared by NMCP (data completeness and data quality), include development and printing of harmonized data collection and M&E tools, monthly data-use and data quality meetings at the prefectural and health facility level, supervisory visits at the prefectural and health facility level to improve malaria data at all levels, dissemination of monthly malaria bulletins, and regular meetings of the M&E technical group, which includes key NMCP and partner staff. PMI will also support standard monitoring activities, including ITN monitoring and therapeutic efficacy monitoring. These activities will be initiated in the coming year per PMI guidance and continue in the next fiscal year.

Proposed activities with FY 2016 funding: *($1,120,000)*

1. *EUV survey:* The semiannual EUV surveys will continue to be implemented to monitor the availability and use of key malaria control commodities at the health facility level on a national scale. Improved logistics management is directly related to the health system's ability to provide effective case management for malaria *($150,000)*;

2. *Health facility survey:* This activity will assess provision of malaria case management services in health facilities. Specific dimensions include health facility readiness to provide services, health worker training and supervision, and health worker performance. The survey will be used to continue to monitor the progress in revitalizing the healthcare delivery system following the Ebola epidemic (i.e., increasing service utilization by the community) *($150,000)*;

3. *Support for 2017 DHS*: PMI will contribute to the 2017 Demographic and Health Survey, the follow up to the 2012 DHS. This survey will provide malaria intervention coverage data and malaria prevalence estimates, both of which can be used to track progress since 2012 and identify high-priority areas for the NMCP *($400,000)*;

4. *ITN durability monitoring:* Prospective long-lasting insecticidal net monitoring will continue to follow ITNs distributed during the 2016 universal coverage campaign, and will provide data on: 1) net survivorship and physical integrity; 2) bioefficacy of insecticides; and 3) insecticidal content *($100,000)*;

5. *Therapeutic efficacy monitoring:* Efficacy monitoring of Guinea's first-line ACT will take place in four sites every two years (two sites in one year and the remaining two sites the following year). The activity will follow WHO's standard protocol. Funds are meant to cover monitoring activities in two sites *($100,000)*;

6. *Routine system strengthening:* Routine system strengthening activities will continue to build upon progress made in M&E training at the district, regional, and national levels, but will be coordinated with a broader health sector effort to strengthen the HMIS. Activities will focus on continuing to ensure the quality of malaria data (including completeness, timeliness, and accuracy) while maximizing data use for decision-making and strengthening the system across health sectors. Specific activities will include the development and harmonization of data collection and M&E tools, monthly meetings at the prefectural and health facility level, quality assurance of malaria data at all levels,

dissemination of monthly malaria bulletins, and support of the M&E technical group *($200,000)*; and

7. *Technical assistance for M&E:* Support for two M&E TDY visits will provide technical assistance for ongoing M&E activities including routine system strengthening, health facility survey, and therapeutic efficacy monitoring. The country team and USAID mission will help define the priority objectives for the TDYs *($20,000)*.

8. Operational research

Guinea does not have any operational research activities.

9. Staffing and administration

Two health professionals serve as resident advisors to oversee PMI in Guinea, one representing CDC and one representing USAID. In addition, one or more Foreign Service Nationals work as part of the PMI team. All PMI staff members are part of a single interagency team led by the USAID Mission Director or his/her designee in country. The PMI team shares responsibility for development and implementation of PMI strategies and work plans, coordination with national authorities, managing collaborating agencies and supervising day-to-day activities. Candidates for resident advisor positions (whether initial hires or replacements) will be evaluated and/or interviewed jointly by USAID and CDC, and both agencies will be involved in hiring decisions, with the final decision made by the individual agency.

PMI professional staff work together to oversee all technical and administrative aspects of PMI, including finalizing details of the project design, implementing malaria prevention and treatment activities, monitoring and evaluation of outcomes and impact, reporting of results, and providing guidance to PMI partners.

The PMI lead in country is the USAID Mission Director. The day-to-day lead for PMI is delegated to the USAID Health Office Director. The two PMI resident advisors, one from USAID and one from CDC, report to the USAID Health Office Director for day-to-day leadership, and work together as a part of a single interagency team. The technical expertise housed in Atlanta and Washington guide PMI programmatic efforts.

The two PMI resident advisors are based within the USAID health office and are expected to spend approximately half their time sitting with and providing technical assistance to the national malaria control programs and partners.

Locally-hired staff to support PMI activities either in ministries or in USAID will be approved by the USAID Mission Director. Because of the need to adhere to specific country policies and USAID accounting regulations, any transfer of PMI funds directly to ministries or host governments will need to be approved by the USAID Mission Director and Controller, in addition to the US Global Malaria Coordinator.

Proposed activities with FY 2016 funding: _($1,162,500)_

1. _USAID technical staff:_ Support one Resident Advisor and one foreign service national to support malaria activities and administration costs _($762,500)_; and
2. _CDC technical staff:_ Support one Resident Advisor to support malaria activities and administration costs _($400,000)_.

Table 1: Budget Breakdown by Mechanism

President's Malaria Initiative – GUINEA

Planned Malaria Obligations for FY 2016

Mechanism	Geographic Area	Activity	Budget ($)	%
TBD – Supply Chain Contract	Nationwide	Procure ITNs, SP, RDTs, ACTs, and microscopes	6,672,500	53%
TBD	Nationwide and PMI target zones	Entomological monitoring, ITN distribution, BCC, training, supervision, diagnostics, capacity building, ITN monitoring, TES, HMIS strengthening	2,916,000	23%
TBD	Nationwide	Capacity development in logistics management, pharmaceutical systems reform, EUV survey and improving drug regulatory capacity	1,300,000	11%
Measure DHS	Nationwide	Support for 2017 DHS for malaria module	400,000	3%
CDC Interagency Agreement	Nationwide	Technical assistance for entomology, community case management, and M&E	49,000	4%
	Conakry	One Resident Advisor	400,000	
USAID/Guinea	Conakry	One Resident Advisor and one locally-engaged staff and support costs for Mission malaria team	762,500	6%
		TOTAL	12,500,000	100%

Table 2: Budget Breakdown by Activity

President's Malaria Initiative – GUINEA

Planned Malaria Obligations for FY 2016

Proposed Activity	Mechanism	Budget		Geographic Area	Description
		Total $	Commodity $		
PREVENTIVE ACTIVITIES					
Insecticide-treated Nets					
Procurement and delivery of ITNs	TBD – Supply Chain Contract	3,060,000	3,060,000	National	Procure and deliver 600,000 LLINs for routine distribution via ANC and EPI clinics.
Distribution of ITNs	TBD	360,000	0	National	Pay for distribution costs of routine nets, calculated at $0.60/net
BCC for ITN use	TBD	Cost covered under BCC section	0	PMI Target Areas	BCC for ITN use will be part of an integrated communication package including MIP and case management, following national standards and in conjunction with what other donors are doing in their respective target areas.
SUBTOTAL ITNs		3,420,000	3,060,000		
Indoor Residual Spraying					

69

Proposed Activity	Mechanism	Budget		Geographic	Description
Entomological monitoring and capacity building	TBD	285,000	0	National	Support for surveillance of vectors and insecticide resistance in each of the four ecological zones; establishment of a permanent insectary and laboratory including procurement of equipment and supplies, capacity building for entomologists, and resources for insectary operations; ITN durability monitoring; and support for NMCP staff (per diems, etc.).
Advanced training for entomological technicians	TBD	40,000	0	National	Four regional technicians based in the sentinel sites will be trained at the Centre Muraz in Bobo-Dioulasso to allow collections of mosquitoes and insecticide resistance tests to be done with reduced supervision from the NMCP.
Technical assistance for entomological capacity building	CDC IAA	29,000	0	National	Funding for two technical assistance visits from CDC to help develop entomological capacity at the national and prefectural level.
SUBTOTAL IRS		354,000	0		
Malaria in Pregnancy					
Treatments of SP	TBD – Supply Chain Contract	187,000	187,000	N/A	Procure approximately 1,565,000 treatments ($0.12 per treatment) of SP to contribute to covering the majority of nationwide needs (580,351 estimated potential pregnancies receiving 3 doses of SP during pregnancy).
Supplies to ensure consumption of SP at ANC	TBD	6,000	6,000	N/A	N/A

Proposed Activity	Mechanism	Budget		Geographic	Description
BCC for IPTp	TBD	Cost covered under BCC section	0	PMI Target Areas	Support BCC to promote ANC clinic attendance and educate pregnant women and communities on the benefits of IPTp. This activity will include support for community-level approaches, such as training of community-based workers as well as mass media (including local radio stations). Immunization outreach sessions will be used as opportunities for educating women. This will be part of a larger integrated BCC activity to satisfy needs for case management, ITNs, and IPTp.
Training/Refresher training for malaria in pregnancy	TBD	Cost covered under Case Management section	0	PMI Target Areas	Provide training and refresher training for public and private health facility midwives and nurses to correctly deliver SP in the context of the focused antenatal care approach. Training will include benchmark assessments, on-the-job training of the new treatment algorithm, and coaching. Training will be part of an integrated training package.
Supervise health workers in IPTp to improve quality of service	TBD	Cost covered under Case Management section	0	PMI Target Areas	On-site supervision for public health facility midwives and nurses to correctly deliver SP in the context of the focused antenatal care approach. Supervision will continue to be part of an integrated approach for supervision at health facilities.
Subtotal Malaria in Pregnancy		193,000	193,000		
SUBTOTAL PREVENTIVE		3,967,000	3,253,000		
CASE MANAGEMENT					
Diagnosis and Treatment					

Proposed Activity	Mechanism	Budget		Geographic	Description
Rapid diagnostic tests (RDTs)	TBD – Supply Chain Contract	2,160,500	2,340,000	National	Procure and distribute approximately 4,155,000 RDTs ($0.52 per test) for use in health facilities and in communities via CHWs.
Microscope consumables	TBD – Supply Chain Contract	20,000	20,000	National	Procure reagents, slides and repair materials for previously purchased microscopes.
AS-AQ	TBD – Supply Chain Contract	675,000	675,000	National	Procure and distribute approximately 1,400,000 ($0.48 per treatment) treatments of AS-AQ.
AL	TBD – Supply Chain Contract	570,000	570,000	National	Procure and distribute approximately 600,000 ($0.95 per treatment) treatments of AL.
Improved malaria diagnostics	TBD	100,000	0	National	Work with the NMCP and National Laboratory to develop and support a comprehensive quality assurance and quality control plan for malaria diagnostics at all levels of the health system. This will include refresher training for lab technicians (and training on malaria microscopy for new laboratory technicians) and regular supervision of microscopy and RDT performance, including systematic review of a predetermined number of positive and negative blood smears and simultaneous use of both tests to assess the quality of RDTs in diagnosing malaria.

Proposed Activity	Mechanism	Budget	Geographic	Description
Training/refresher training in RDT use and case management	TBD	325,000	PMI Target Areas	Training in RDT use, malaria case management, and malaria in pregnancy for health workers at hospitals, health centers, and health posts who have not been trained using previous years funds. Also, M&E training for district and regional level officials. Training of CHWs not yet trained in RDT use, in treatment of uncomplicated malaria and referral for patients with severe malaria, as well as referral of pregnant women to ANCs. Continue implementation of a comprehensive refresher training schedule for health workers and CHWs who have already received initial training.
		0		
Supervision of health workers and CHWs in RDT use and case management	TBD	250,000	PMI Target Areas	Enhanced clinical supervision at all levels of the health care system, including hospitals, health centers, health posts, and CHWs. District Health Team staff (*Département Préfectoral de Santé*) and regional health team staff (*Département Régional de Santé*) will be actively involved in supervision activities, along with health center staff for supervision of CHWs. Supervision visits will include observation of patient consultations and feedback to providers.
		0		

73

Proposed Activity	Mechanism	Budget		Geographic	Description
BCC for case management	TBD	Cost covered under BCC section	0	PMI Target Areas	Funds will be used to support integrated behavior change communication and education activities for communities to improve behaviors related to malaria prevention and treatment. The BCC supported will target prevention activities, including use of ITNs and IPTp. BCC activities will also support appropriate care seeking behaviors; particularly at the community level through use of CHWs. Emphasis will be placed on prompt care-seeking for fever and other symptoms of malaria.
Community case management	TBD	500,000	0	PMI Target Areas	Support the scale-up of community case management in PMI target areas, including management and logistic costs, and support for data management, as well as training and supportive supervision of 650 CHWs.
Subtotal Diagnosis and Treatment		4,600,500	3,605,000		
Pharmaceutical Management					
Improving logistic management information systems	TBD	250,000	0	National and Regional Level	Continued support to strengthen the Logistics Management Information System to enable the pharmaceutical system collect, compile and process consumption data throughout the health system in order to improve the forecasting, the procurement and the distribution of commodities. Includes procurement of computers, support for Internet connectivity, capacity building for quantification at the central level (PCG, DNPL) as well as at the regional, prefectures and district levels.

Proposed Activity	Mechanism	Budget		Geographic	Description
Pharmaceutical systems reform	TBD	200,000		National	Continue to support the reform of regulations governing the supply chain management system, including advocacy for signing a convention between the Government and PCG and improvement of the governance of PCG (renewal and functioning of the board, information sharing, civil society and private sector's participation, etc.).
Improve drug regulatory capacity	TBD	100,000		National	Continue to support improvement of the regulatory and oversight capacities of the DNPL, revision of national list of essential drugs and enhanced control of compliance to the pharmaceutical policy and regulations by PCG and the private pharmacies network.
Management of pharmaceutical supplies	TBD	300,000		National	Manage the distribution of PMI commodities down to the health facility level, including warehousing, transportation, storage and distribution.
Strengthen pharmaceutical storage capacity	TBD	300,000		National	This activity will build on current PMI's support to PCG to provide additional equipment and material to improve commodities storage conditions at the central level as well as at regional level.
Subtotal Pharmaceutical Management		1,150,000	0		
SUBTOTAL CASE MANAGEMENT		5,750,500	3,605,000		
HEALTH SYSTEM STRENGTHENING / CAPACITY BUILDING					

75

Proposed Activity	Mechanism	Budget	Geographic	Description
Management support for NMCP	TBD	150,000	National and Prefectural Levels	Support to the NMCP to assist them in team building, logistics and supervision, office management including communication capacity/connectivity, and M&E systems strengthening.
Training of NMCP staff	TBD	50,000	National and Prefectural Levels	Support to NMCP to build capacity via conference and workshop attendance, both national and international, to improve program management in M&E as well as BCC.
SUBTOTAL HSS & CAPACITY BUILDING		200,000		
BEHAVIOR CHANGE COMMUNICATION				
BCC for ITNs, IPT, and case management	TBD	300,000	PMI Target Areas	BCC will be part of integrated communication package including ITN use and MIP and will include case management at both the facility and community levels, following national standards and in conjunction with what other donors are doing in their respective target areas. This activity will be implemented in health districts targeted by PMI, using the NMCP communication plan.
SUBTOTAL BCC		300,000		
MONITORING AND EVALUATION				
End-use Verification	TBD	150,000	National	The semiannual EUV surveys will continue to be implemented to monitor the availability and use of key malaria control commodities at the health facility level on a national scale. Improved logistics management is directly related to the health system's ability to provide effective case management for malaria.

Proposed Activity	Mechanism	Budget	Geographic	Description
Health facility survey	TBD	150,000	National	This activity will assess provision of malaria case management services in health facilities. Specific dimensions include health facility readiness to provide services, health worker training and supervision, and health worker performance. The survey will be used to continue to monitor the progress in revitalizing the healthcare delivery system following the Ebola epidemic.
Support for 2017 DHS	MEASURE DHS	400,000	National	PMI will contribute to the 2017 Demographic and Health Survey, the follow up to the 2012 DHS. This survey will provide data on coverage data for malaria interventions, and will also provide malaria prevalence estimates which can be used to track progress since 2012, as well as identify high-priority areas for the NMCP.
ITN durability monitoring	TBD	100,000	National	Prospective ITN monitoring will continue to follow ITNs distributed during the 2016 universal coverage campaign, and will provide data on: 1) net survivorship and physical integrity; 2) bioefficacy of insecticides; and 3) insecticidal content.
Therapeutic efficacy monitoring	TBD	100,000	National	Efficacy monitoring of Guinea's first-line ACT will take place in four sites every two years (two sites in one year and the remaining two sites the following year). The activity will follow WHO's standard protocol. Funds are meant to cover monitoring activities in two sites.

Proposed Activity	Mechanism	Budget		Geographic	Description
Routine system strengthening	TBD	200,000		National	Routine system strengthening activities will continue to build upon progress made in M&E training at the district, regional, and national levels, but will be coordinated with a broader health sector effort to strengthen the HMIS. Activities will focus on continuing to ensure the quality of malaria data (including completeness, timeliness, and accuracy) while maximizing data use for decision-making and strengthening the system across health sectors. Specific activities will include the development and harmonization of data collection and M&E tools, monthly meetings at the prefectural and health facility level, quality assurance of malaria data at all levels, dissemination of monthly malaria bulletins, and support of the M&E technical group.
Technical assistance for M&E	CDC IAA	20,000		National	Support for two M&E TDY visits will provide technical assistance for ongoing M&E activities including routine system strengthening, health facility survey, and therapeutic efficacy monitoring. The country team and USAID mission will help define the priority objectives for the TDYs.
SUBTOTAL M&E		1,120,000	0		
OPERATIONS RESEARCH					
SUBTOTAL OR		0	0		
IN-COUNTRY STAFFING AND ADMINISTRATION					
CDC	CDC IAA	400,000	0		Support for one USAID PMI Advisor and one

Proposed Activity	Mechanism	Budget		Geographic	Description
USAID	USAID	762,500	0		USAID locally-engaged senior malaria specialist as well as one CDC PMI Advisor, and all related local costs to sitting in USAID Mission.
SUBTOTAL IN-COUNTRY STAFFING		1,162,500	0		
GRAND TOTAL		**12,500,000**	**6,858,000**		

Table 2: Budget Breakdown by Activity
President's Malaria Initiative – GUINEA
Planned Malaria Obligations for FY 2016
Revised March 24, 2016

Proposed Activity	Mechanism	Budget Total $	Budget Commodity $	Geographic Area	Description
PREVENTIVE ACTIVITIES					
Insecticide-treated Nets					
Distribution of ITNs (routine)	TBD	387,000	0	National	Pay for distribution costs of routine nets, total amount will need to be reviewed based on amount of nets going to PMI zones.
Distribution of ITNs (mass campaign)	Stop Palu	3,033,000	0	PMI Target Areas	Cover distribution costs for 2016 universal coverage campaign (early release)
BCC for ITN use	TBD	Cost covered under BCC section	0	PMI Target Areas	BCC for ITN use will be part of an integrated communication package including MIP and case management, following national standards and in conjunction with what other donors are doing in their respective target areas.
SUBTOTAL ITNs		3,420,000	0		
Indoor Residual Spraying					
Entomological monitoring and capacity building	TBD	285,000	0	National	Support for surveillance of vectors and insecticide resistance in each of the four ecological zones; establishment of a permanent insectary and laboratory including procurement of equipment and supplies, capacity building for entomologists, and resources for insectary operations; ITN durability monitoring; and support for NMCP staff (*per diems*, etc.).
Advanced training for entomological technicians	TBD	40,000	0	National	Four regional technicians based in the sentinel sites will be trained at the Centre Muraz in Bobo-Dioulasso to allow collections of mosquitoes and insecticide resistance tests to be done with reduced supervision from the NMCP.
Technical assistance for entomological capacity building	CDC IAA	29,000	0	National	Funding for two technical assistance visits from CDC to help develop entomological capacity at the national and prefectural level.
SUBTOTAL IRS		354,000	0		
Malaria in Pregnancy					
Treatments of SP	TBD-Supply Chain Contract	187,000	187,000	N/A	Procure approximately 1,565,000 treatments ($0.12 per treatment) of SP to contribute to covering the majority of nationwide needs (580,351 estimated potential pregnancies receiving 3 doses of SP during pregnancy).
Supplies to ensure consumption of SP at ANC	TBD	6,000	6,000	N/A	N/A

Activity	Funding	Cost (1)	Cost (2)	Location	Description
BCC for IPTp	TBD	Cost covered under BCC section	0	PMI Target Areas	Support BCC to promote ANC clinic attendance and educate pregnant women and communities on the benefits of IPTp. This activity will include support for community-level approaches, such as training of community-based workers as well as mass media (including local radio stations). Immunization outreach sessions will be used as opportunities for educating women. This will be part of a larger integrated BCC activity to satisfy needs for case management, ITNs, and IPTp.
Training/Refresher training for malaria in pregnancy	TBD	Cost covered under Case Management section	0	PMI Target Areas	Provide training and refresher training for public and private health facility midwives and nurses to correctly deliver SP in the context of the focused antenatal care approach. Training will include benchmark assessments, on-the-job training of the new treatment algorithm, and coaching. Training will be part of an integrated training package.
Supervise health workers in IPTp to improve quality of service	TBD	Cost covered under Case Management section	0	PMI Target Areas	On-site supervision for public health facility midwives and nurses to correctly deliver SP in the context of the focused antenatal care approach. Supervision will continue to be part of an integrated approach for supervision at health facilities.
Subtotal Malaria in Pregnancy		193,000	193,000		
SUBTOTAL PREVENTIVE		3,967,000	193,000		
CASE MANAGEMENT					
Diagnosis and Treatment					
Rapid diagnostic tests (RDTs)	TBD-Supply Chain Contract	2,160,500	2,160,500	National	Procure and distribute approximately 4,155,000 RDTs ($0.52 per test) for use in health facilities and in communities via CHWs.
Microscope consumables	TBD-Supply Chain Contract	20,000	20,000	National	Procure reagents, slides and repair materials for previously purchased microscopes.
AS-AQ	TBD-Supply Chain Contract	675,000	675,000	National	Procure and distribute approximately 1,400,000 ($0.48 per treatment) treatments of AS-AQ.
AL	TBD-Supply Chain Contract	570,000	570,000	National	Procure and distribute approximately 600,000 ($0.95 per treatment) treatments of AL.
Improved malaria diagnostics	TBD	100,000	0	National	Work with the NMCP and National Laboratory to develop and support a comprehensive quality assurance and quality control plan for malaria diagnostics at all levels of the health system. This will include refresher training for lab technicians (and training on malaria microscopy for new laboratory technicians) and regular supervision of microscopy and RDT performance, including systematic review of a predetermined number of positive and negative blood smears and simultaneous use of both tests to assess the quality of RDTs in diagnosing malaria.

Activity	Partner			Location	Description
Training/refresher training in RDT use and case management	TBD	325,000	0	PMI Target Areas	Training in RDT use, malaria case management, and malaria in pregnancy for health workers at hospitals, health centers, and health posts who have not been trained using previous years funds. Also, M&E training for district and regional level officials. Training of CHWs not yet trained in RDT use, in treatment of uncomplicated malaria and referral for patients with severe malaria, as well as referral of pregnant women to ANCs. Continue implementation of a comprehensive refresher training schedule for health workers and CHWs who have already received initial training.
Supervision of health workers and CHWs in RDT use and case management	TBD	250,000	0	PMI Target Areas	Enhanced clinical supervision at all levels of the health care system, including hospitals, health centers, health posts, and CHWs. District Health Team staff (*Département Préfectoral de Santé*) and regional health team staff (*Département Régional de Santé*) will be actively involved in supervision activities, along with health center staff for supervision of CHWs. Supervision visits will include observation of patient consultations and feedback to providers.
BCC for case management	TBD	Cost covered under BCC section	0	PMI Target Areas	Funds will be used to support integrated behavior change communication and education activities for communities to improve behaviors related to malaria prevention and treatment. The BCC supported will target prevention activities, including use of ITNs and IPTp. BCC activities will also support appropriate care seeking behaviors; particularly at the community level through use of CHWs. Emphasis will be placed on prompt care-seeking for fever and other symptoms of malaria.
Community case management	TBD	500,000	0	PMI Target Areas	Support the scale-up of community case management in PMI target areas, including management and logistic costs, and support for data management, as well as training and supportive supervision of 650 CHWs.
Subtotal Diagnosis and Treatment		4,600,500	3,425,500		
Pharmaceutical Management					
Improving logistic management information systems	TBD	250,000	0	National and Regional Level	Continued support to strengthen the Logistics Management Information System to enable the pharmaceutical system collect, compile and process consumption data throughout the health system in order to improve the forecasting, the procurement and the distribution of commodities. Includes procurement of computers, support for Internet connectivity, capacity building for quantification at the central level (PCG, DNPL) as well as at the regional, prefectures and district levels.

Activity	Coverage	Partner	Amount	Amount	Description
Pharmaceutical systems reform	National	TBD	200,000	0	Continue to support the reform of regulations governing the supply chain management system, including advocacy for signing a convention between the Government and PCG and improvement of the governance of PCG (renewal and functioning of the board, information sharing, civil society and private sector's participation, etc.).
Improve drug regulatory capacity	National	TBD	100,000	0	Continue to support improvement of the regulatory and oversight capacities of the DNPL, revision of national list of essential drugs and enhanced control of compliance to the pharmaceutical policy and regulations by PCG and the private pharmacies network.
Management of pharmaceutical supplies	National	TBD	300,000	0	Manage the distribution of PMI commodities down to the health facility level, including warehousing, transportation, storage and distribution.
Strengthen pharmaceutical storage capacity	National	TBD	300,000	0	This activity will build on current PMI's support to PCG to provide additional equipment and material to improve commodities storage conditions at the central level as well as at regional level.
Subtotal Pharmaceutical Management			1,150,000	0	
SUBTOTAL CASE MANAGEMENT			5,750,500	3,425,500	
HEALTH SYSTEM STRENGTHENING / CAPACITY BUILDING					
Management support for NMCP	National and Prefectural Levels	TBD	150,000	0	Support to the NMCP to assist them in team building, logistics and supervision, office management including communication capacity/connectivity, and M&E systems strengthening.
Training of NMCP staff	National and Prefectural Levels	TBD	50,000	0	Support to NMCP to build capacity via conference and workshop attendance, both national and international, to improve program management in M&E as well as BCC.
SUBTOTAL HSS & CAPACITY BUILDING			200,000	0	
BEHAVIOR CHANGE COMMUNICATION					
BCC for ITNs, IPT, and case management	PMI Target Areas	TBD	300,000	0	BCC will be part of integrated communication package including ITN use and MIP and will include case management at both the facility and community levels, following national standards and in conjunction with what other donors are doing in their respective target areas. This activity will be implemented in health districts targeted by PMI, using the NMCP communication plan.
SUBTOTAL BCC			300,000	0	
MONITORING AND EVALUATION					

Activity	Partner	Amount		Scope	Description
End-use Verification	TBD	150,000	0	National	The semiannual EUV surveys will continue to be implemented to monitor the availability and use of key malaria control commodities at the health facility level on a national scale. Improved logistics management is directly related to the health system's ability to provide effective case management for malaria.
Health facility survey	TBD	150,000	0	National	This activity will assess provision of malaria case management services in health facilities. Specific dimensions include health facility readiness to provide services, health worker training and supervision, and health worker performance. The survey will be used to continue to monitor the progress in revitalizing the healthcare delivery system following the Ebola epidemic.
Support for 2017 DHS	MEASURE DHS	400,000	0	National	PMI will contribute to the 2017 Demographic and Health Survey, the follow up to the 2012 DHS. This survey will provide data on coverage data for malaria interventions, and will also provide malaria prevalence estimates which can be used to track progress since 2012, as well as identify high-priority areas for the NMCP.
ITN durability monitoring	TBD	100,000	0	National	Prospective ITN monitoring will continue to follow ITNs distributed during the 2016 universal coverage campaign, and will provide data on: 1) net survivorship and physical integrity; 2) bioefficacy of insecticides; and 3) insecticidal content.
Therapeutic efficacy monitoring	TBD	100,000	0	National	Efficacy monitoring of Guinea's first-line ACT will take place in four sites every two years (two sites in one year and the remaining two sites the following year). The activity will follow WHO's standard protocol. Funds are meant to cover monitoring activities in two sites.
Routine system strengthening	TBD	200,000	0	National	Routine system strengthening activities will continue to build upon progress made in M&E training at the district, regional, and national levels, but will be coordinated with a broader health sector effort to strengthen the HMIS. Activities will focus on continuing to ensure the quality of malaria data (including completeness, timeliness, and accuracy) while maximizing data use for decision-making and strengthening the system across health sectors. Specific activities will include the development and harmonization of data collection and M&E tools, monthly meetings at the prefectural and health facility level, quality assurance of malaria data at all levels, dissemination of monthly malaria bulletins, and support of the M&E technical group.

			National	
Technical assistance for M&E	CDC IAA	20,000	0	Support for two M&E TDY visits will provide technical assistance for ongoing M&E activities including routine system strengthening, health facility survey, and therapeutic efficacy monitoring. The country team and USAID mission will help define the priority objectives for the TDYs.
SUBTOTAL, M&E		1,120,000	0	
OPERATIONS RESEARCH				
SUBTOTAL, OR		0	0	
IN-COUNTRY STAFFING AND ADMINISTRATION				
CDC	CDC IAA	400,000	0	Support for one USAID PMI Advisor and one USAID locally-engaged senior malaria specialist as well as one CDC PMI Advisor, and all related local costs to sitting in USAID Mission.
USAID	USAID	762,500	0	
SUBTOTAL IN-COUNTRY STAFFING		1,162,500	0	
GRAND TOTAL		12,500,000	3,618,500	